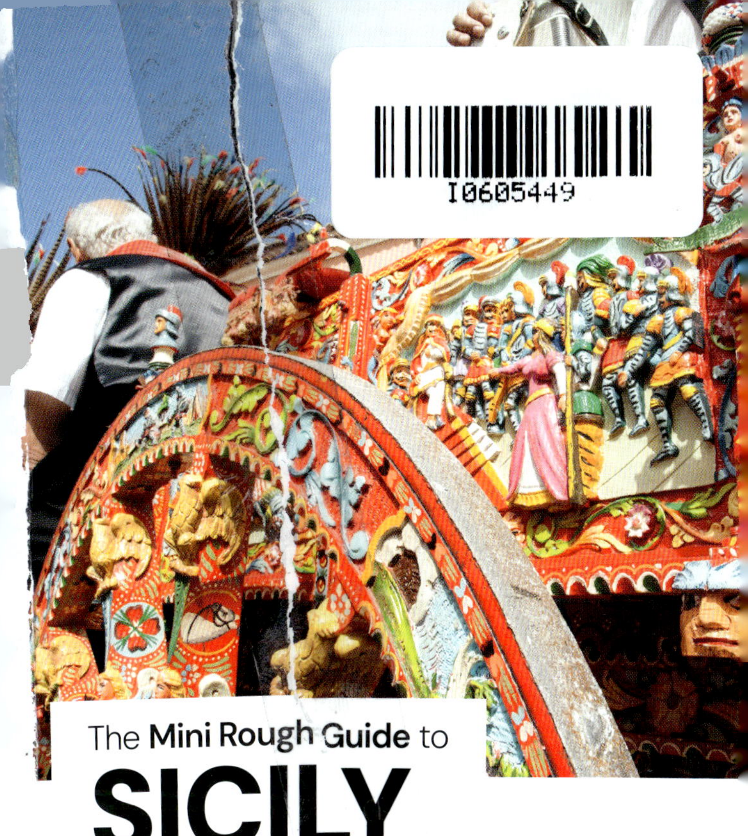

The **Mini Rough Guide** to

SICILY

ROUGH GUIDES

HOW ROUGHGUIDES.COM/TRIPS WORKS

STEP 1

Pick your dream destination, tell us what you want and submit an enquiry.

STEP 2

Fill in a short form to tell your local expert about your dream trip and preferences.

STEP 3

Our local expert will craft your tailor-made itinerary. You'll be able to tweak and refine it until you're completely satisfied.

STEP 4

Book online with ease, pack your bags and enjoy the trip! Our local expert will be on hand 24/7 while you're on the road.

PLAN AND BOOK YOUR TRIP AT
ROUGHGUIDES.COM/TRIPS

How to download your Free eBook

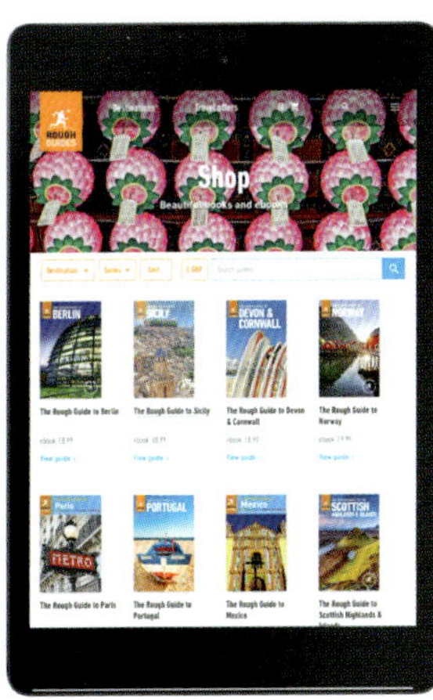

1. Visit **www.roughguides.com/free-ebook** or scan the **QR code** opposite

2. Enter the code **sicily051**

3. Follow the simple step-by-step instructions

For troubleshooting contact: mail@roughguides.com

Contents

Introduction

When Sicilians make the 3km (2 mile) trip across the Strait of Messina, they are likely to say that they are going to Italy or 'il continente'. Italians living on the peninsula, likewise tend to think of their neighbours in Sicily as being different – a distinction with which few Sicilians would take issue. In many ways the digital era has strengthened Sicilian identity. From street food outlets and artisan bakeries, home restaurants and farm-stays to prickly pear jam and T-shirts bearing (often rude) slogans in dialect, social media has provided a platform for Sicilians committed to revaluing their unique heritage Travellers will quickly notice that Sicily feels different from Italy. To understand why, you need only look to the past. For over 3,000 years, just about all the powers that sailed – and battled to control - the Mediterranean, set their sights on Sicily.

The sighs of their presence are tangible. Classical Greek temples, mosaic-filled Norman churches and ornate Baroque piazzas lends a theatrical and decidedly unique presence to the island. In Palermo, the cathedral richly ornamented by the Spanish is only steps away from the mosaic-filled palace that was the seat of the enlightened courts of the island's Saracen and Norman rulers; the Baroque churches and piazzas of Catania incorporate columns of Roman temples; medieval Erice is built near the site of a temple to Venus allegedly erected by some of the island's earliest settlers, the Elymians, on

NOTES

Sicily is a great destination for adventurous visitors. Coast, islands and mountains lend themselves to year-round sporting activities, from hiking up mountains and volcanoes to scuba diving and snorkelling in marine reserves, gorge trekking and exploring offshore islands. At a stretch you could even ski on Etna in the morning and sun yourself on the coast in the afternoon.

their return from the Trojan wars

Many islanders still speak dialect as well as Italian, a combination of words and sounds from the long Greek, Latin, Aragonese, Arabic and Norman-French past. Sicilian is so incomprehensible to most Italians that Sicilian films and TV series have to be subtitled. The food in Sicily is different from that of the mainland, too: the lemons, capers and almonds that the Arabs brought with them from North Africa still appear in many dishes. Since most Sicilians don't live far from the sea, fish, often the *pesce spada* (swordfish) caught in the Strait of Messina, is a staple on most menus.

Orange picking in Catania

Sicilian way of life

Travellers will probably notice that Sicilians approach life a little differently than other Italians do. It is difficult to quantify exactly what these differences are, but being among Sicilians is one of the pleasures of touring the island. They are welcoming to their visitors, and are likely to strike up a conversation about a son who studied in London or a cousin who lives in Chicago or Brooklyn. Indeed perhaps it is because almost a third of the island's population emigrated in the late 19th and early 20th century, that Sicilians, understanding how it is to be a stranger in a strange land, are so welcoming.

WHAT'S NEW

The magnificently restored Palazzo Butera – home to the world-class Valsecchi collection of contemporary art opened in Palermo in 2022. You could happily spend an entire day exploring the palace and its collection, taking a break for a fine lunch in the gallery's wonderful restaurant, Le Cattive. Milazzo, the main port for the Aeolian Islands, is experiencing a gastronomic boom, with gourmet gelato (at Sikè), cornetti filled with ricotta made from the farm's buffalo at Tenuta Anasita, and the recent opening of Trattoria del Esposito, where locally sourced ingredients appear on a reasonably priced fixed menu. As for trends, Taormina is flourishing in the wake of the HBO series, *The White Lotus*, filmed in the San Domenico Palace hotel, fresh from a make-over by Four Seasons. Ortigia is on the way to becoming another Taormina, with new bars, restaurants and boutiques opening every month. In Noto, the Rocco Forte group are opening a new hotel in Palazzo Castelluccio, following the roaring success of their spectacular rescue of the Villa Igieia in Palermo.

A diverse island

Sicily is the largest island in the Mediterranean, a hefty 25,708 sq km (9,926 square miles), and its landscapes of tall mountains, vast coastal plains and inland valleys are more diverse than those of many countries. The Sicilian scenery is dramatic, sometimes harsh but seldom graceless. Nor is the island short on natural spectacle.

Mount Etna, Europe's most forceful volcano, is also Sicily's tallest mountain and most famous natural wonder. It dominates, and periodically threatens, the eastern coast. The Madonie are rugged mountains that rise behind the northern coast, and Capo San Vito, a rocky headland etched with beaches and secluded coves, is at the island's northwestern tip. The volcano on Stromboli, one of the Aeolian Islands that float off the northern coast, can be counted on to provide a round-the-clock performance: it sends fiery lava down the mountainside into the hissing sea about every half hour. In the southeast, are dramatic limestone gorges, honeycombed with caves, such as Cava Grande and Pantalica.

Topping a short and by no means inclusive list of cultural sights to include on even the briefest tour would be Agrigento, Selinunte and Segesta, with the largest and best-preserved Greek temples on the island, if not in Europe. Cefalù, on the northern coast, and Taormina, on the eastern coast, are justifiably the island's most popular seaside resorts. Aside from their beaches, these pleasant towns also throw in some remarkable monuments: a Greek theatre and medieval palaces in Taormina, a Norman cathedral and an Arabic old town in Cefalù. Erice, on the west coast, is the most dramatically poised town on the island, perched atop the rocky escarpment of a tall mountain high above windmill-studded salt pans and the sea.

Mount Etna

Ancient cities and towns

Palermo, the capital, is on the northern coast, and Catania, the island's second largest city, is on the eastern coast. Beyond the unattractive modern outskirts of both are old centres filled with monuments that include Norman remnants in Palermo and Baroque churches and piazzas in Catania – both charged with urban vitality.

WHEN TO GO

Unless you like extremely high temperatures (48 degrees was recorded in Sicily in 2022) and sardine-packed beaches, avoid July and August, when much of the Italian population are on holiday. September is still hot – though the weather can be a little unsettled – and when Italian schools open towards the middle of the month, things quieten down considerably. September, October and even November can be fantastic times to be in Sicily – the sea is still warm, but it is cool enough to do some intensive sightseeing. Winter can be crisp and sunny -- a good time to visit major tourist centres without the crowds and with the locals. Spring is beautiful – the countryside carpeted with wildflowers – though the weather can be a bit unsettled, and the sea takes a long time to warm up.

In the southeastern corner of the island is an unusually satisfying collection of cities and towns. Siracusa, the most powerful centre of Greek Sicily, is here, and several of its ancient ruins lie among the tangle of medieval alleyways and Baroque that form its islanded centre, Ortigia. Inland from Siracusa, are the UNESCO-listed towns designed in the unrestrained style of Sicilian Baroque following an earthquake that devastated this corner of Sicily in 1693. Of them, Noto takes the prize for architectural fantasy. A little deeper into the interior, nestling among oak and hazel woods is the little village of Casale near Piazza Armerina. Here, at the Villa Romana, are some of the most extensive Roman floor mosaics ever uncovered anywhere.

Regeneration

Travellers will come to Sicily with some notions of the island's ongoing woes, most notably the activities of the Mafia, or else Cosa Nostra. In recent years, however, the Mafia has begun to lose its grip. Genuine grassroots movements have seen a growing number of small businesspeople refuse to pay *pizzo* (protection money) while the confiscation of Mafia property – and its redevelopment in a socially and environmentally sensitive way – continues apace. The refusal to support the Mafia in many quarters is just part of Sicily's present: throughout the island churches and palaces have been restored and sketchy downtown areas revived, while an ever-increasing number of chic city and hip country house hotels and restaurants have made Sicily an attractive destination for the most sophisticated traveller.

Cala Tonnarella dell'Uzzo

SUSTAINABLE TRAVEL

Electric cars are not widely available to rent, but e-bikes and e-scooters are becoming increasingly common, and charging points are more frequent. Hydrofoils serving the minor islands have reduced their speed to reduce emissions, resulting in slightly longer journeys. In a nation where everyone drinks bottled water, redesigning plastic bottles so that the lids remain attached makes some difference in the amount of plastic left on beaches, and many bars are now happy to refill metal water bottles. More and more hotels are committed to reducing their impact on the planet through measures ranging from installing solar panels to avoiding single-use plastic by using refillable containers for bathroom products.

10 Things not to miss

1 **AEOLIAN ISLANDS**
Visit these lovely volcanic islands by hydrofoil. See page 53.

2 **MOUNT ETNA**
You can take a train around Sicily's smoking volcano. See page 60.

3 **VALLEY OF THE TEMPLES**
Sicily's most breathtaking ancient site, at Agrigento. See page 79.

4 **VILLA ROMANA**
Many of the finest Roman mosaics ever uncovered are here in Casale. See page 65.

5 **PARCO ARCHEOLOGICO DELLA NEAPOLIS**
Contains the fascinating remains of the ancient city of Syracuse. See page 68.

6 **MONREALE**
The cathedral here glitters with spectacular mosaics on every surface. See page 47.

7 **NOTO**
The quintessential Sicilian Baroque town, full of extravagant ornamentation. Ed: current pic still works unless you can change to monster balcony of palazzo villadorata. See page 77.

8 **CEFALÙ**
A popular resort on the north coast, with a sandy beach and attractive old town. See page 49.

9 **TAORMINA**
A charming hillside town whose extraordinary views have been astonishing travellers for centuries. See page 57.

10 **RISERVA DELLO ZINGARO**
Set on the rugged coastline west of Palermo, this beautiful nature reserve has fabulous walks, beaches and birdlife. See page 90.

A perfect tour of Sicily

DAY 1

Taormina. This is Sicily's most sophisticated resort, in a dramatic setting overlooking Mount Etna. Treat yourself to a stay in one of its iconic grand hotels; amble along the Corso soaking up the views, and lunch on fresh seafood by the beach at the Villa Sant'Andrea hotel. Take a dip in the sea, then check out evening drama, music and film at the Greek Theatre.

DAY 2

Mount Etna. Join a 4-wheel drive or trekking tour from Taormina to explore the foothills of Etna. Return to Taormina for sunset cocktails and volcano views.

DAY 3

Catania. Ignore the urban sprawl and enjoy the vibrant centre with its street markets and grandiose palazzi and churches. Lunch at the atmospheric Osteria Antica Marina in the fish market.

DAY 4

Siracusa. Head south to Siracusa. Visit the Archaeological Park of Neapolis, then take a bus or taxi to explore the seductive island of Ortigia. A short boat trip around the island later, join the *passeggiata* (evening stroll) along the seafront, then have an *aperitivo* on Lungomare Alfeo.

DAY 5

Val di Noto. Explore the World Heritage Baroque cities of the Val di Noto. Start at Noto, whose Corso Vittorio Emanuele is flanked by glorious Baroque palazzi and churches. Take a dip at the Lido di Noto, or the quieter Riserva Naturale di Vendicari, with sandy beaches and a wealth of birdlife. Drive to Modica and combine sightseeing with retail therapy (excellent shops here) and gastronomy.

DAY 6

Scicli and Ragusa. Spend a leisurely morning in Scicli, a beautiful little Baroque town, wandering along picturesque Via Mormino Penna. Drive north to Ragusa, following signs for Ragusa Ibla, where old world charm prevails. Explore the beautifully restored town, then treat yourself to dinner in one of its two Michelin star restaurants, Locanda Don Serafino or Ristorante Duomo.

DAY 7

Agrigento. Head west to Sicily's greatest archaeological site, Agrigento's Valley of the Temples. Wander among evocative Greek temple ruins and then cool off in the Kolymbetra Gardens. Dine at Ex Panificio in modern Agrigento, then join the locals strolling along Viale della Vittoria.

DAY 8

Enna and Villa Romana. Head inland to the hill town of Enna. Drive south to Villa Romana del Casale to see the finest in-situ Roman floor mosaics in existence.

Sicily for foodies

DAY 1

Palermo's markets. Spend a day grazing on local street food such as *pane e pannelle* (bread rolls with chickpea fritters) and shopping for produce to take home from the local markets.

DAY 2

Cooking lesson. The next day, learn to cook Sicilian style with a Duchess in the palace that once belonged to Giuseppe Tomasi di Lampedusa, author of *The Leopard*.

DAY 3

The Aeolian Islands. Head to the island of Salina to taste sweet Malvasia and an ever-expanding range of dry wines at wineries such as Hauner and Caravaglio. Take the local bus to Pollara, to visit Sapori Eoliani, the island's leading producer of salted capers – as well as salted capers, buy some candied capers.

DAY 4

Caper tasting. Pick up the bus again and head down to Rinella to sample the candied capers paired with ricotta granita at Papero, then move on to Lingua for a 'salina' *pane cunzato* (toasted bread piled high with caper pesto, tomatoes, ricotta, mint and grilled aubergines).

DAY 5

Fish market. Witness the best fish market in Sicily – then eat some at the traditional market trattoria, Antica Marina. Refresh your palate with a fizzy seltz – lemon juice with salt and soda water – from one of the little kiosks dotted around the centre.

DAY 5

Bronte. Drive to Bronte, the capital of the pistachio, best sampled in the pastries and ices sold in cafes along the main street. Dine on pasta with pistachio pesto at one of the simple local trattorias.

DAY 6

Etna. Tour vineyards on Etna North – such as Franchetti and Cornelissen – looking out as you drive for roadside stalls selling apples and pears, hazelnuts and chestnuts. Treat yourself to a night at the Monaci delle Terre Nere hotel, for a fine meal that makes the best of local produce.

DAY 7

Modica & Scicli. See how chocolate is made at historic producer Bonajuto, then sample a hot chocolate at one of the bars along the main Corso. Stock up on chocolate for presents – flavours range from jasmine to cinnamon and chilli. Drive over to the nearby town of Scicli for the evening *passeggiata* as you work your way through the fabulous ice creams made by the Nivera gelateria from carefully sourced Sicilian ingredients, on Via Mormino Penna. Head back to Modica for dinner – opting for the Modica speciality, ravioli stuffed with ricotta and dressed in a rich pork *ragù*.

Sicily's great outdoors

DAY 1

Ustica. Ustica is the best place in Sicily for diving – the seabed holds both natural and archeological wonders. There are several excellent diving schools, and their guided dives are the best way of making sure you don't miss anything. On shore, you can walk around the entire island in a few hours.

DAY 2

Vulcano. Climb the active volcano of Vulcano, then wallow in the warm sulphurous mud baths and swim over bubbling fumaroles. Take an afternoon boat trip from Lipari or Salina that includes swimming above columns of volcanic bubbles off Panarea and an ascent of Stromboli.

DAY 3

Salina. On Salina, climb the mountain of Monte Fossa delle Felci, then take an evening guided walk along the paths of Valle Spina to watch the sunset. Head torches are provided for the walk back to the village of Leni. Take a hydrofoil to Filicudi, where boat trips will take you snorkelling in sea caves.

DAY 4

Mount Etna and Gole dell'Alcantara. Explore Mount Etna guided by a volcanologist, then head to the Gole dell'Alcantara where a river flows between spectacular volcanic rock formations. In summer the river is wade-able – an unforgettable experience.

DAY 5

Cava Grande del Cassibile. Hike down to the bottom of this magnificent limestone gorge with caves, waterfalls and natural pools you can swim in. There are several trails – one of the best is called Mastra Ronna. Finish your day with a swim from the sandy beach of Marchesa di Cassibile.

DAY 6

Pantalica. The magnificent gorge of Pantalica is home to Sicily's largest and most fascinating ancient necropolis, with several thousand Neolithic tombs honeycombing its sheer limestone cliffs. The river Anapo runs through it (with several places to swim), and the most straightforward path follows the line of a former railway along its banks. Early spring is the best time to come – look out for locals gathering wild asparagus!

DAY 7

Madonie. The Madonie mountain range rising to the south of Cefalù is an enticing area of beech and pinewoods, flower-filled upland plains, craggy rocks, undulating foothills, high passes and soaring peaks (including the highest mountains in Sicily after Etna). The highest peak is Pizzo Carbonara (1979m), but a more varied hike is along Sentiero #10 from Portella Ferrone (outside the pretty village of Petralia Soprana) to Piano Catarineci with magnificent views right across the Madonie to the Aeolian Islands.

History

All roads may lead to Rome, but for much of recorded history all sea lanes have led to Sicily. The island's position, strategically sited in the middle of the Mediterranean, has been both the proverbial curse and a blessing. Sicilians haven't enjoyed too many centuries of peace, but the various powers that coveted and ruled their island over the centuries left behind a heady mix of cultures and riches.

The Greeks, Romans and Carthaginians turned the island into one of the great powerbases – and food-producers – of ancient times; the Arabs brought culture and transformed the land with irrigation technology perfected in the deserts; then the Normans routed the Saracens, and the Spanish stepped in to replace the French.

The Phoenicians left a remarkable settlement, Mozia, on the little island of San Pantaleo, off the western coast, while Sicily's Ancient Greek cities, especially those at Siracusa, Agrigento, Selinunte and Segesta, provide us with some of the best-preserved architectural remnants to come down from the classical age. The sumptuous mosaics at Casale are the most spectacular relics of the Romans, who were here until the last days of the Empire; and the Cappella Palatina in Palermo, and the cathedrals at Monreale and Cefalù, show off the considerable achievements of the Normans, who came to Sicily from the lands of northern France. The Castello Ursino in Catania is an example of the fortifications required to defend a foothold in Sicily during the Middle Ages.

NOTES

The main reason the Phoenicians came to Sicily was because the shallow waters of the western coast were a superb source of murex, a marine mollusk whose glands, when dried, produced a precious purple dye – the Imperial Purple that was a symbol of power in ancient Greece and Rome.

Temple of Concord, Valley of the Temples

Early settlers

Long before these empires began to establish strongholds in Sicily, Paleolithic and Neolithic peoples were occupying settlements scattered across the island. By the 10th century BC, a tribe known as the Sicels had migrated from mainland Italy to Sicily, giving the island its name. The Sicels settled in the east; the Sicani, from North Africa, and the Elymians, thought to have descended from the Trojans, established themselves in the west.

Sometime around the 8th century BC, Phoenicians sailed from the shores of the eastern Mediterranean to establish outposts at Mozia and along the western coast. The Greeks, who would eventually overpower all these cultures, began arriving on the eastern coast about the same time. Most of the Greek settlers came in search of land to farm, and Sicily offered vast tracts of fertile soil and ideal

NOTES

Although in general usage the word 'tyrant' implies someone oppressive and cruel, in the Ancient world the word existed more as a title which declared a man to be the absolute ruler of a Greek colony, and probably someone who had seized power – not unlike today's dictators. Some tyrants, like Theron, father-in-law of Gelon of Siracusa, were considered wise and fair.

growing conditions. From colonies in Siracusa and elsewhere along the east coast, the Greeks spread across the island, establishing colonies at Gela, Agrigento and Selinunte. Agrigento, known to the ancients as Akragras, became especially powerful, and enough is left of this city on the southern coast to suggest the extent of its wealth. However, Siracusa soon became the supreme power on Sicily.

The Greek centuries

In 480 BC, the armies of the various Greek colonies joined forces under Gelon, the tyrannical ruler of Siracusa, to defeat the Carthaginians at Himera, on Sicily's northern coast. The Greek victory ensured the supremacy of Siracusa in the affairs of Sicily until the city fell to the Romans some 250 years later. The victory also assured that Sicily would become a major Greek power in the Mediterranean; in fact, Sicily and the southern Italian mainland became known as Magna Graecia (Greater Greece) and had a larger Greek population – and at times more influence -- than Greece itself.

Greek dominance, however, didn't bring an end to warfare. The colonies often fought among themselves. Segesta, an Athenian satellite in the northwestern, was almost continually at war with Selinunte, an ally of Siracusa on the coast, 60kim away. Athens was alarmed by the ambitions of Siracusa and saw an opportunity to attack when Segesta asked for help in repelling the attacks from

Selinunte. Athens assembled a massive fleet and sailed to Sicily in 415 BC; but the so-called Great Expedition ended in a humiliating defeat for the Athenians. The Siracusans imprisoned some 7,000 Athenian soldiers and put them to work in its limestone quarries, the Latomie.

Carthage, the colony the Phoenicians settled on the north shore of Africa near modern-day Tunis, wasn't as easy to quell. The Carthaginians attacked Selinunte, Agrigento and other Sicilian cities. Siracusa's tyrannical ruler, Dionysius I, retaliated in 397 BC by levelling Mozia, the Carthaginian stronghold on the island. Under Agathocles, Sicilian troops crossed the Mediterranean and attacked the Carthaginians on their own turf.

In the 3rd century BC, Sicily became the battleground of the Punic Wars that broke out between Rome and Carthage. When Siracusa sided with the Carthaginians in the Second Punic War, Rome sacked the city in 211 BC and took control of the island. The Roman Empire continued to control Sicily for the next seven centuries.

Detail of Triumph of Death fresco at Palazzo Abatellis

Romans and the Saracens

For Rome, Sicily was one vast wheat field, supplying the Empire with grain. For the most part Roman rule

Castle in Erice

brought a commodity that until then was unknown in Sicily – peace, as well as the amphitheatres, baths and other Roman structures that still stand around the island.

Christianity arrived in Sicily around AD 200, and Siracusa became one of the most fervent early Christian strongholds in the Mediterranean, thousands of Siracusans worshipping and burying their dead in catacombs beneath the city until the Emperor Constantine lifted the prohibition against Christians a century later. Not long after Rome fell to the Visigoths in 410, Sicily became prey to Vandals and Ostrogoths who sacked the coasts. By 535 the island had fallen into the hands of the Byzantines; Siracusa was capital of the Eastern Byzantine Empire for five years, from 663 to 668.

The next wave of invasion came from North Africa. The island of Pantelleria, where an Arabic influence is still much in evidence, fell first in 700. It wasn't until the 9th century that the assault began in force. After decades of fighting, the so-called Saracens – including Arabs, Spanish Muslims and Berbers – took Palermo in 831 and Siracusa in 878. Arab rule ushered in another golden age for Sicily. Palermo became one of the largest and most cosmopolitan cities in the world, comparable to Constantinople and Baghdad. The Muslim rulers revitalised the countryside, building irrigation systems and introducing oranges and lemons to the landscape.

MASTERS OF A SICILIAN STYLE

While the achievements of Greeks and Normans are often what capture a visitor's attention, Sicilian artists have made considerable contributions of their own – several artists developed a distinctly Sicilian style in their work. You will encounter them frequently around the island.

Domenico Gagini (1448–1492) came to Palermo in 1458 and spent the rest of his life gracing churches with his elegant Madonnas and other sculptures; his son, **Antonello** (1478–1536), carried on the tradition by becoming Sicily's foremost sculptor of the Renaissance. You will find their work in numerous churches and in Palermo's Galleria Regionale della Sicilia, where a room is filled with Gagini masterpieces.

Rosario Gagliardi (1700–1770) is the architect who created many of the Baroque churches and public buildings that transform towns like Noto and Ragusa into stage sets. The church of San Giorgio in Ragusa is a fine example of his mastery of this whimsical style.

Antonello da Messina (1430–1479) combined a mastery of light and spatial depth to create such masterpieces as his *Portrait of an Unknown Man*, now in the Museo Mandralisca in Cefalù, and The Annunciation, in the Museo Bellomo in Palermo.

Giacomo Serpotta (1656–1732) perfected the art of stucco work, or moulded plaster. His creations, which adorn the Oratorio del Rosario di San Domenico and other oratorios in Palermo, cover the walls with delicate religious imagery.

Puppet shows in Sicily date back centuries

Once again, the prosperity of Sicily proved to be irresistible to other powers. This time it was a Norman lord, Roger de Hauteville, who set his sights on the island and took Messina in 1061. All of Sicily was under Norman rule by 1091, with Palermo as its capital and Roger as its ruler. Rather than impose a foreign yoke on the island, Roger accommodated the island's rich Greek, Roman, Byzantine and Roman heritage – Norman art and architecture, so richly preserved in the Norman churches in Palermo, Monreale and Cefalù, displays this fusion. When Roger's son was crowned Roger II, King of Sicily, in 1130, his holdings included Sicily and most of southern Italy and his court was one of the wealthiest and most cosmopolitan in the world.

Stupor Mundi and the Sicilian Vespers

A descendant, Frederick II von Hohenstaufen, was to carry on the Norman tradition of enlightened rule when he took the crown in 1220. He introduced a unified legal system, promoted the arts and sciences and encouraged a blending of Islamic, Jewish and Christian cultures. Frederick ruled for more than 40 years and became known as *Stupor Mundi*, the Wonder of the World.

Frederick's death once again left Sicily up for grabs. Among the contenders was the Papacy under Pope Urban IV, eager to get control of the lands of southern Italy. Backed by the Pope, Charles of Anjou, brother of the French King Saint Louis (Louis IX), defeated the Hohenstaufen supporters in a series of battles and became King of Sicily and Naples in 1268. Determined to punish Sicily for its loyalty to the Hohenstaufens, Charles imposed heavy taxes and confiscated lands.

An uprising against French rule broke out in Palermo on 30 March 1282; the first shots rang out at the hour the bells of the church of Santo Spirito rang for Vespers, and the revolt has come to be known as the Sicilian Vespers. Some claim that it was instigated by the Byzantine Emperor Michael VIII, who had learned that Charles was plotting to attack Constantinople, and wished to divert the French by keeping them busy in Sicily. The immediate cause was an incident in which a French soldier stopped a Sicilian bride on her way to church and searched her for concealed weapons. An angry crowd killed the soldier immediately, and within days the citizenry had slaughtered more than 8,000 French troops across the island.

King Peter III of Aragon (whose wife, Constance, was a Hohenstaufen) arrived in a flotilla five months later, and the Sicilian nobles offered the Spaniard the throne. The Angevins and the Aragonese skirmished for control of the island for a tumultuous 20 more years, and in the end, Sicily ultimately ended up belonging to the Spanish – and would remain safely in their hands for the next 400 years.

NOTES

The Mafia took root in Sicily in the 1860s, ostensibly to help the rural poor have their share of the land reform and other benefits that were to accompany freedom from rule. In effect, the Mafia became an integral part of the island's power structure, controlling business and the workings of government, and today is said to ensure that Sicily remains a centre for drug trafficking.

Spanish rule

Sicily became more or less a backwater when the European powers directed their expansionist ambitions to the New World. This inattention ensured that Sicily enjoyed one of the few periods of long peace in its history. In the absence of human drama, nature stepped in. The plague, brought to Sicily by the ships that called at its harbours, broke out repeatedly and decimated large portions of the population.

The end of the 17th century was especially calamitous. Mount Etna erupted in 1669 and sent molten lava flowing through the streets of Catania. An earthquake in 1693, also centred in the east, was even more destructive and took an enormous toll on human life. Sicilians rebuilt Noto and other cities in a distinctive style, the Sicilian Baroque.

The Treaty of Utrecht divided Spanish holdings, and in the early 18th century Sicily once again became a pawn of foreign powers. The island passed from the Italian House of Savoy to the Austrians and, in 1734, back to the Spanish, this time to the Bourbons. The British convinced the Bourbon king Ferdinand I to introduce a constitution, but he soon repealed it and called in Austrian mercenaries when citizens took to the streets of Palermo and other cities calling for independence; his successor, Ferdinand II, bombarded Messina in 1848 to quell an uprising for independence there.

From unification into the present

This unrest set the stage for Giuseppe Garibaldi, leader of the Risorgimento, the campaign for the unification of Italy. He sailed into Marsala on 11 May 1860 with his so-called Thousand, a reference to the guerrilla army that accompanied him. Garibaldi's soldiers and Sicilian partisans were soon fighting in Palermo, and the island was free of Bourbon rule within a year. Sicilians were soon disillusioned – widespread poverty and government repression made life as part of a unified Italy more difficult than it had been under the Bourbons.

The Monument to Giuseppe Garibaldi , Trapani

For many Sicilians, the only escape from impoverishment was emigration. By 1914, more than a million and a half Sicilians had left the island, usually for North and South America. The reforms introduced later by Mussolini and his fascist government did little to alleviate poverty, illiteracy and unemployment in Sicily.

The island once again became a battleground in World War II. In July 1943, the Allies made their first European landings at Gela on the southern coast while British and Canadian forces tackled the east coast. Allied bombardments flattened Messina, where the German defensive was entrenched. Other cities were not spared. In fact, World War II bombsites are still visible in parts of central Palermo.

The postwar years saw the rise of the Mafia, as government and international funds for rebuilding, were siphoned off to finance more nefarious activities. In the early 1980s, a Mafia war left

Palermo's streets strewn with blood and the Corleone-based clan the undisputed victors. In 1992 two anti-Mafia magistrates were murdered. The terror continued with bombs in Milan and Rome that killed innocent bystanders. The revulsion sparked in Sicilians by these assassinations weakened the Mafia's grip on public opinion and dented the age-old code of loyalty (*omertà*). A grassroots association (Addiopizzo) was set up to fight against the payment of the *pizzo*, protection money, and since it was founded hundreds of businesses across Sicily have signed up.

Chronology

Before 10,000 BC Paleolithic and Neolithic peoples settle in the Egadi Islands.
10th century BC Sicels, Sicani and Elymians settle in Sicily.
8th century BC Phoenicians establish outposts at Mozia; Greek colonists settle in Gela, Agrigento and Selinunte.
480 BC The Greeks defeat the Carthaginians. Siracusa becomes Sicily's most powerful city.
211 BC Following Second Punic War, Rome takes control of Sicily.
c.200 AD Early Christianity takes hold in Sicily.
663–668 Siracusa now capital of eastern Byzantine Empire.
9th century Saracens take Palermo and Siracusa to rule Sicily.
11th century Roger de Hauteville brings Sicily under Norman rule.
1220 Frederick II von Hohenstaufen, of Norman and Swabian heritage, takes the crown and brings 40 years of enlightened rule to Sicily.
1268 Charles of Anjou becomes King of Sicily and Naples.
30 March 1282 The Sicilian Vespers uprising ousts the French and installs the Spanish.
1693 An earthquake flattens cities in the southeast; in rebuilding, the flamboyant style of Sicilian Baroque is created.
1734 Sicily passes to the Spanish house of Bourbon.
11 May 1860 Giuseppe Garibaldi sails into Marsala; Sicilians oust the Bourbons to become part of the new Kingdom of Italy.

Late 19th–early 20th centuries Many Sicilians emigrate.
July 1943 Allies make first European landings of World War II in Sicily.
1951-1975 One million Sicilians emigrate.
1968 An earthquake in the Belice Valley leaves 50, 000 people homeless.
1980s–1990s Mafia violence triggers government crackdown and citizen movements against organised crime.
2022 Right-wing Giorgia Meloni elected prime minister.
2023 Mafia boss Matteo Messina Denaro arrested, after being on the run for 30 years, and dies in jail nine months later.
2024 Following an agreement with Libya and Tunisia, small boat crossings to Sicily fall for the first time.

The Highland Division landing in Sicily, July 1943

The historic town of Modica

Places

The easiest way to see a good measure of Sicily's cities, ruins, beaches and other attractions is to circle the coast and make occasional forays into the interior and to nearby islands. We begin in Palermo, and head east to start a tour.

Palermo

Highlights

- **The Quattro Canti**, see page 34
- **The Albergheria**, see page 36
- **The Cattedrale and Palazzo dei Normanni**, see page 37
- **From the Vucciria to Piazza Verdi**, see page 39
- **La Kalsa**, see page 42
- **Around Palermo**, see page 45

Palermo ❶ may not instantly enchant its visitors. The chaotic capital of Sicily is noisy, traffic-filled and riddled with decay in parts, overbuilt with concrete in others. But take your time, and you'll discover a truly fascinating and multi-layered city. Begin with the pedestrianised artery, Via Maqueda, lined with casual contemporary Sicilian spots for a snack or drink, then begin to explore the narrow streets and alleys of the old city. You'll discover Norman palaces, Baroque churches, chapels shimmering in mosaics, outdoor markets overflowing with olives and blood oranges, quaint puppet theatres and grandiose

NOTES

Only 90 minutes by hydrofoil from Palermo, a day trip to the lovely neighbouring island of Ústica is an enjoyable excursion. As Sicily's first protected marine reserve, it is understandably popular with swimmers and scuba divers.

oratories; and a great deal of warm-hearted street life. Restoration of palaces and churches, and the requalification of entire quarters – such as La Kalsa and Ballarò – continues, while since 2015, Palermo's Arab-Norman monuments (together with the cathedral churches of Cefalù and Monreale) have been recognised as UNESCO World Heritage sites.

The Quattro Canti

The **Quattro Canti** Ⓐ, or Four Corners, is a buzzy – and recently pedestrianised – crossroads at the centre of the old city that divides it into four *quartiere*, quarters; most of Palermo's sights are an easy walk from this busy junction, the intersection of the Via Maqueda and the Corso Vittorio Emanuele. The façades of the buildings on each corner here – three Baroque palazzi and the church of **San Giuseppe dei Teatini** – are ornamented with fountains, and each is also embellished in turn with statuary that represents a season, one of four Spanish kings of Sicily and the patron saint of one of the four quarters that surround the Quattro Canti. If the church is open, step inside for a look at the angels, stuccoes, frescoes and other ornamentation that are typical of the Sicilian Baroque.

In Piazza Pretoria, Palermo

Piazza Pretoria Ⓑ is just a few steps south along Via Maqueda. The **Fontana Pretoria** takes up most of the square and in more puritan times was nicknamed the Piazza della Vergogna, or Square of Shame – this being a reference to the seeming licentiousness of the naked figures who frolic in the spray. More than 30 naked or near-naked nymphs, tritons, gods and youths of varying sizes and quality surround the fountain's vast circular basin. Garibaldi is said to have sat on the edge of the fountain during the fierce battles of 1870, instilling the citizenry with the courage to fight on for independence. Flanking one side of the square is the **Palazzo delle Aquile**, the town hall, named for the stone eagles that decorate its façade. The other massive presence is the church of **Santa Caterina**; behind its austere façade is another Baroque interior, covered with brightly coloured frescoes and plasterwork angels that tumble from every surface. Follow signs to the Convento di Santa Caterina where you can sit in a leafy cloister with coffee in paper cups and a lavish cake or pastry which the nuns here have been making since the Bourbon kings were on the throne.

> **NOTES**
>
> Nuns, it is said, chopped off the noses of the statues of naked men in Piazza Pretoria but stopped short of castration. The noses have been restored and ornamental railings now ensure no one gets too close.

Piazza Bellini, just a few steps to the east, is graced with the three small red domes of the chapel of **San Cataldo** Ⓒ (charge) and the 12th-century campanile of **La Martorana** Ⓓ. (charge). San Cataldo is squat and plain, and aside from its mosaic flooring, was left undecorated when its founder, a chancellor of William I, died in 1160. La Martorana is more elaborate, and was founded by George of Antioch, Roger II's chief minister, in 1146 as a seat of the Greek Orthodox church. Despite a Baroque restoration that added the

Palermo's Cathedral

cupids around the entryway, much of the Norman mosaic work remains intact. The gold, green and azure tiles of the dome depict Christ flanked by saints and prophets, and a nearby mosaic of Christ crowning Roger II is said to be a reliable likeness of the Norman king.

The Albergheria

The streets and alleys of the Albergheria quarter, once the home of Norman court officials and rich merchants from Pisa and Amalfi, stretch south and west of Piazza Bellini. Via Maqueda and Via Bosco lead into the centre of the quarter, the Piazza Carmine, passing stately palaces, centuries-old buildings that show their age and even the occasional rubble-filled site left by World War II bombings. The stalls of the **Mercato di Ballarò** Ⓔ, Palermo's liveliest daily market, fill Piazza Carmine, the adjacent Piazza Ballarò and the surrounding streets. It is raucous, sprawling and exotic, with mountains of lemons and oranges, slabs of tuna and swordfish, pigs' trotters and intestines. Above this busy scene rises the green-and-white dome of **Chiesa del Gesù**, founded in the late 16th century as the first Jesuit church in Sicily, and that of the church of the **Carmine**. While the interior of Il Gesù is another swirl of Baroque excess, that of the Carmine is vast and far more sedate. To gain a sense of how the area is gentrifying, explore the streets around Piazza Santa Chiara – and don't miss the Arab water tower on Piazzetta Sette Fate.

The Cattedrale and Palazzo dei Normanni

From Quattro Canti, Corso Vittorio Emanuele leads west past shops and Baroque palaces to several of Palermo's most important monuments. The first is the **Cattedrale** **F** (http://cattedrale.palermo.it; charge) that was begun in 1185 but not completed, with the addition of a dome, until 1801. As a result, the building is an incongruous mixture of styles: the 12th-century towers are Norman, the façade and south porch are Gothic and the interior is coldly Neoclassical.

The church is a pantheon of the Normans, who came to Sicily in 1061, routed the Arabs and ruled the island ably for a century. Roger II, the Norman king who made the island the centre of the Mediterranean World, was interred here among his royal relations against his will: he wanted to be buried in the cathedral he built in Cefalù (see page 49). In the adjacent Treasury, Constance of Aragon's bejewelled crown is on display alongside rings and other artefacts removed from the royal tombs during a 19th-century rearrangement. Of a more macabre nature are the relics of several saints, including a withered extremity said to be the foot of Mary Magdalen.

A short distance away is the **Palazzo dei Normanni**, or Palazzo Reale, that actually was built by Sicily's

Glittering mosaics in the Palatine Chapel

Arab rulers in the ninth century. Under both the Arabs and the Normans, Palermo was one of the largest and most civilised cities in the world and the palace was a centre of the arts and learning.

Little of the Arab and Norman palace remains: the façade that overlooks the old city is a 17th-century addition made by the island's Spanish rulers, and many of the salons and lesser quarters are now occupied by Sicily's regional government. One stunning Norman remnant, however, is the **Cappella Palatina** **G** (www.federicosecondo.org; charge), the exquisite chapel commissioned by Roger II. Mosaics cover every surface, depicting the tales of the Old and New Testaments in a frank, charming style that infuses the softly lit space with a sense of faith and earnest artistry executed for the love of God and a just ruler. Capping the glittering profusion of gold and silver tiles is a purely Arab touch: a honeycombed, wooden ceiling.

A marble staircase leads from the chapel to the Royal Apartments. The best room, in a small wing of the original Norman palace, is the Sala di Re Ruggero. The walls are covered in mosaics of hunting scenes and exotic landscapes.

STREET MARKETS

In the narrow winding lanes at the heart of Palermo are the bustling markets of Ballarò and Capo; these are where the locals shop every day for fresh, Sicilian produce. There is an abundance of meat, fish and local vegetables and fruit as well as, in many of the side streets, clothes, household goods and any amount of bootleg watches and designer bags. It's fun to explore and shop here; stalls offering cheeses, salamis and cold meats are ideal for creating a picnic lunch, though many of the offerings at the 'street food' stalls should be avoided by those who don't like their food to have been sitting uncovered in the sun all day. As in street markets everywhere, be aware that pickpockets and jewellery snatchers may be looking for opportunities.

San Giovanni degli Eremiti

Another remnant of Norman Palermo, the now deconsecrated church of **San Giovanni degli Eremiti** **H** sits just south of the palace on Via dei Benedittini. While the interior is stark and devoid of elaborate decoration, this five-domed Norman-Arab church is beautiful in its simplicity and is surrounded by gardens and cloisters planted with palms, cactus and jasmine. The **Parco d'Orléans** across the street is named for the one-time resident of the palace it surrounds: Louis-Philippe d'Orléans, who was exiled here in 1809 in the aftermath of the Paris Commune and later returned to France to become King. The palace is now the residence of the Regional President.

Oratorio di Santa Cita

From the Vucciria to Piazza Verdi

Corso Vittorio Emanuele leads northeast from Quattro Canti towards the sea and several other quarters of old Palermo. Just a few blocks from the Quattro Canti, the Corso crosses Via Roma, which slightly north skirts what was once the most famous market in Palermo, **Vucciria**, now a shadow of its former self **I**.

A few blocks north of the market, Via Roma comes to **Piazza San Domenico**, an airy square dominated by the 18th-century façade of the church of the same name. Behind the church is the remarkable **Oratorio del Rosario** Ⓙ (donation). Some of Palermo's best Baroque artistry decorates small chapels like this one, in which stucco cherubs and other figures cover every inch of the walls. The Rosario is the finest of all, since its exuberance is the work of the master of Baroque decoration Giacomo Serpotta, a native of Palermo. The altarpiece is a rich depiction of the Virgin of the Rosary by Van Dyck; the Dutch painter came to work in Palermo's churches sometime around 1628, but he left when the plague broke out and completed this painting in Genoa.

More of the friezes that emerged from Serpotta's fertile imagination and skilled hands also decorate the **Oratorio di Santa Cita** Ⓚ (donation), a few blocks north on Via Squarcialpo. Stucco angels surround frescoed stories from the New Testament and spectacular scenes depicting the victory of the Christian fleets over the Turks at the Battle of Lepanto.

Teatro Massimo in Palermo

The Museo Archeológico

The recently revamped **Museo Archeológico Regionale** Ⓛ (www.coopculture; charge) is on the other side of Via Roma. In rooms surrounding the two cloisters of a former monastery, some of the most important pieces unearthed in Sicily are displayed alongside finds from elsewhere in the ancient world: painting

WHERE TO SHOOT THE BEST PICTURES

There's a photo opportunity every which way you turn in Sicily. Beguiling Mount Etna, Europe's highest and most active volcano, with eerie craters and bubbling lava fields, offers incredible views from the summit that lure adventurous photographers. You can also head to Piano Provenzana for impressive panoramic mountain shots. The volcanic Aeolian Islands are another first choice for envy-inducing photographs, especially during spring when the wildflowers blanket the ground. However, sometimes, the small and everyday day affords the best photographs. Lively street scenes in throbbing Palermo, colourful markets (like Ballarò) and contrasting architectural styles. And then there are the historic sights, best photographed early in the morning (and off-season) to avoid crowds. Explore the golden-hued churches of Noto, the ancient ruins of Siracusa or the atmospheric Valley of the Temples in Agrigento for breathtaking scenes of ancient Sicily.

fragments from Pompeii, Roman bronzes, Greek vases, a room floored with Roman mosaics uncovered in Palermo and an extensive collection of Etruscan urns and tombs, found in Tuscany.

The prize exhibits, though, are the pieces from Selinunte, the ruined city on Sicily's southwestern coast (see page 82). A famed collection of metopes, the stone carvings that adorned the tops of the temples around 470 BC, is towards the back of the museum in the eastern wing that is entirely devoted to **Selinunte**. Several figures from Greek mythology appear on the reliefs. In one, Perseus beheads Medusa, and in another, dogs set upon Acateon.

Teatro Massimo

The museum is only a block east of the centre of the modern city, the Piazza Verdi. This busy piazza was laid out in the 19th century and is now surrounded by modern office blocks and designer shops. At the centre of the square is the **Teatro Massimo** Ⓜ (www.teatromassimo.it), opened in 1897 and one of the grandest opera

GETTING AROUND PALERMO

Palermo is well served with public buses and getting to other parts of Sicily from here by bus, coach or train is relatively simple.

Municipal buses are cheap and easy to use. There's a flat fare valid for 90min, or you can buy an all-day ticket. Buy them from AMAT (http://amat.pa.it) booths outside Stazione Centrale, at the southern end of Viale della Libertà, in *tabacchi* and anywhere else you see the AMAT sign, or from the driver for a small supplement. Validate tickets in the machine at the back of the bus as you board – spot checks are carried out by plainclothes inspectors.

Palermo's Metropolitana metro service was created for commuters passing through Stazione Centrale and only has 16 stations. It is not really useful for visitors wishing to see the city.

houses in Europe. It has an enormous stage and seats 3,400 for performances of ballet, concerts and opera. What's most remarkable about this domed Neoclassical structure is the fact that its massive doors are once again open: the theatre was hidden behind weeds and scaffolding for almost a quarter of a century. It reopened to much fanfare in 1997, exactly a hundred years after the huge stage was inaugurated with a production of Verdi's *Aida*. Tickets to performances here are always in high demand.

La Kalsa

Palermo's oldest district extends southeast from the intersection of Via Roma and Corso Vittorio Emanuele. The Arabs settled this seaside quarter in the 10th century, and later, Sicilian aristocrats built fine residences along the narrow streets. Today it is a picturesque quarter, full of places to eat and drink.

San Francesco and San Lorenzo

Via Alessandro Paternostro leads south off the Corso to the **Chiesa di San Francesco d'Assisi** Ⓝ, a large Gothic structure with a sparse, stone interior that pays just tribute to Italy's patron saint. When decoration does intrude, it does so gently, most notably in the Cappella Mastrontonio. Here, a sculpted arch by Francesco Laurana frames the entrance and is the earliest known Renaissance work in Sicily. The nearby **Oratorio di San Lorenzo** is another masterpiece of decoration by Giacomo Serpotta and is also famous for a lost artwork: a *Nativity* by Caravaggio, stolen in 1969 and never recovered.

Piazza Marina

The Corso continues north to the seaside and soon skirts **La Cala**, the restored harbour, now full of swish yachts. On the landward side, **Piazza Marina** ❿ contains the Giardino Garibaldi where locals play dominoes and cards under banyan trees. The regenerated piazza is flanked by open-air bars and restaurants and overlooked by handsome palazzi. The restored **Palazzo Steri** also known as Palazzo Chiaramonte (www.coopculture.it; charge) is a Catalan-Gothic fortress most famous as the headquarters of the Inquisition from 1685 to 1782. Recently restored, it now includes several museums, including an armoury and a prison as well as being home to Renato Guttuso's iconic painting of La Vucciria market. After passing through

Display at Palermo's Puppet Museum

Banyan trees at the Orto Botanico

the Porto Felice, the Corso ends at the new **Foro Italico** Ⓟ seafront and a vista of the gulf with Monte Pellegrino rising in the background. This was Palermo's grand seafront in the days of the Belle Époque; the area fell into decline and stayed there until the creation of the promenade. The waterfront now features gardens and pathways popular with joggers, soccer-players and sunbathers.

Via Butera, just inside the walls, is lined with some of the city's best-preserved palaces. One of them houses the **Museo Internazionale delle Marionette** (www.museodellemarionette.it; charge), with a collection of exotic puppets that provide an introduction to this still-popular Sicilian entertainment. Via Butera is also home to the extraordinary contemporary collection of **Massimo Valsecchi** Ⓠ (www.palazzobutera.it; charge) in Palazzo Butera which opened in 2022 after a ground-breaking restoration project that had the international art world marvelling. The philosophy behind the palazzo is that visitors should come in and look at whatever draws them, whether it be the art or the palazzo itself, rather than seeking out the most famous works.

Galleria Regionale at Palazzo Abatellis

Around the corner, on Via Alloro, is the **Galleria Regionale** Ⓡ (https://turismo.comune.palermo, charge) where paintings and sculpture fill the rooms of the 15th-century **Palazzo Abatellis**. The first floor is devoted to sculpture. Several works are by Franceso Laurana, whose sculpted archway graces the nearby church of San Francesco (see page 42) his masterpiece here is a bust of Eleonora of Aragon. Another room is devoted to Antonello Gagini and other members of this family who dominated Sicilian Baroque sculpture for much of the 15th and 16th centuries. The palace chapel is decorated with *The Triumph of Death* by an unknown mid-15th century artist; the eponymous subject is an archer who, from the back of a horse, launches his arrows at the noble and meek alike, sparing no one the inevitable end. Sicilian paintings hang in the upstairs galleries, with among them several fine works by Antonello da Messina.

Via Vetriera leads south from the museum to Piazza Kalsa, and just beyond this rather derelict square are two other leafy retreats. The gardens of the **Villa Giulia** and the adjoining **Orto Botanico** ⓢ (http://ortobotanico.unipa.it; charge) were laid out in the late 18th century and are abloom with tropical vegetation that surrounds pools and pavilions.

Catacombe dei Cappuccini

Around Palermo

On the outskirts of Palermo are a number of palaces, churches and other sights which the city's public transport network puts within easy reach of the centre.

La Zisa

When the Norman King William I began to build this retreat in 1160, he fashioned the gardens and palace in the manner of an Arab pleasure pavilion. **'La Zisa'** (www.coopculture.it; charge) comes from the Arabic *el aziz*, or magnificent, and the mosaics, arches, fountains, vaulted ceilings and lattice windows of the three-floor palace reveal the opulence that once prevailed here. The palace later became a fortress and grand residence before returning to its Moorish roots. Now restored, with the Moorish gardens reinstated, La Zisa is magnificent once more.

Catacombe dei Cappuccini

In the various niches and rooms of the **Catacombe dei Cappuccini**, (http://catacombepalermo.it; charge) beneath a Capuchin monastery, are the clothed corpses of 8,000 men, women and children. Many of them look remarkably alive – over the years the monks perfected a technique of injecting corpses with chemicals and dyes. The practice of preserving the dead in this fashion died out in 1920.

Parco della Favorita and Monte Pellegrino

On the northern edge of Palermo, the woods and formal gardens of the **Parco della Favorita** climb the lower slopes of Monte Pellegrino. Ferdinand III, Bourbon King of the Two Sicilies, chose this hilly terrain as his place of exile in 1799, and installed himself in the eccentric **Palazzina Cinese** (free). Now restored, this Oriental folly combines Chinese decorative motifs with both Gothic and Egyptian flourishes. Next door, the **Museo Etnografico Siciliano Pitrè** houses an ethnographic collection illustrating Sicilian life, customs and folklore.

Higher up the mountain is the **Sanctuario di Santa Rosalia**, a cave-turned-chapel that is Palermo's popular pilgrimage site. Allegedly, Palermo was saved from the plague in 1624 when

Rosalia, the hermit niece of King William II, appeared to a peasant in a vision and told him to find her remains here and give her a proper burial.

Monreale

The best example of Norman art and architecture is not in Palermo, but in the hillside town of **Monreale** ❷, 13km (8 miles) to the southeast. William II started the town's cathedral in 1174 – allegedly after the Madonna appeared to him in a vision and instructed him to do so, though it was more likely that he was motivated by political reasons. William had broken ties with Walter of the Mill, Bishop of Palermo; Walter was building a new church, the

Monreale Cathedral

Cefalù

present-day Palermo cathedral, and William set out to outdo him. He succeeded.

The **Cattedrale Monreale**, (http://monrealeduomo.it; charge) set high above the Conca d'Oro valley and Palermo, was completed in just ten years and is one of the great monuments of the Middle Ages. Inside, the dome, walls and columns shimmer with 130 large mosaics – perhaps the finest example of mosaic art in the world. They tell the stories of the Old and New Testaments and surround *Christ Pantocrator* (Christ the Almighty), about 6 metres (20ft) tall, that dominates the central apse.

Among the many saints portrayed in the mosaics is Thomas Becket. It was William's father-in-law, Henry II of England, who had martyred Becket but the church, meanwhile, had canonised Becket the year before the cathedral was begun, so by honouring him William was casting his allegiance with the powerful papacy. William and his father are buried in the south chapel, not far from the entrance to the **cloisters** that were part of the monastery that stood here originally. You can reach Monreale 8km (5 miles) away on bus 389 from Palermo's Piazza Indipendenza.

Villa Cattolica retains its grandeur and houses the Museo Guttoso, a bizarre collection of contemporary paintings and the tomb of Sicilian painter Renato Guttoso (1912–87).

Mondello

Palermo's most popular getaway, **Mondello** ❸ (its full name is Partanna-Mondello) follows a long sandy beach beneath the northern flanks of Monte Pellegrino. The rocky, forested bluffs of the mountain and the headlands of Capo Gallo at the northern end of the beach lend the town a sense of remote beauty; the fishing harbour and little lanes that wind around a medieval clock tower provide the atmosphere of a small Mediterranean fishing village. The town is liveliest in the evening, when Palermitani come out to Mondello for a seaside *passeggiata* (evening stroll) and a meal in the town's many fish restaurants. You can join them by taking bus 806 from Piazza Politeama.

East from Palermo

Highlights

- **Cefalù**, see page 49
- **Into the Madonie**, see page 51
- **Tindari**, see page 52
- **The Aeolian Islands**, see page 53

The coast east of Palermo is richly endowed with old towns, ancient ruins, rugged mountains, fine beaches and, not far offshore, a volcanic archipelago. Since many of these places lie on or near the main railway lines, they can be reached easily from Palermo; or, you might consider making Cefalù your base and exploring the surrounding attractions from there.

Cefalù

Cefalù ❹, 70km (42 miles) east of Palermo, would be a remarkable place even without the twin-towered cathedral that rises high above its red-tile roofs. This magnificent structure, founded by Roger II in 1131, is itself overshadowed by a massive crag that crowds the church and the town between a wall of rock and the sea.

Museo Mandralisca

Allegedly, Roger was caught at sea in a storm and vowed to build a cathedral at the first harbour he came upon. That harbour was Cefalù, which by then had already witnessed the passing of the Carthaginians, Greeks, Byzantines and Arabs. Their presence is noted in the dusty collections of the **Museo Mandralisca**, (http://fondazionemandralisca.it; charge) where the relics on display include a rare Greek vase depicting tuna fishing in the Aeolian Islands. The treasure, though, is *Portrait of an Unknown Man*, Antonello da Messina's rendering of a sly-smiled, enigmatic man who is often compared to the Mona Lisa. This collection and the palace were bestowed to the town by the 19th-century Baron Enrico Mandralisca, by all accounts a remarkable man who devoted his life to the study of natural history and archaeology and served in the first Italian Parliament.

On the beach in Cefalù

Piazza Duomo and the Old Town

The **cathedral** (https://duomocefalu.it/en; charge) is on the Piazza Duomo, in the centre of town, its Norman interior splendid with Byzantine mosaics. High above the central apse is *Christ Pantocrator*, with an elongated face and powerful eyes that seem to follow a visitor around the church; the Bible he holds is open to Latin and Greek inscriptions of 'I am the light of the world'. He is surrounded by the Virgin Mary and the twelve apostles. Among the other sparse ornamentation that remains is a *Madonna and Child*, by Sicilian master Antonello Gagini.

From the piazza, narrow alleys lead into the old town and to some appealing relics of Cefalù's past. The old Greek walls provide a nice view over the sea and the town, and the *lavatoio* is a wash house from the Arab days. Many of the streets end as staircases that descend to the old harbour, where a stone wharf juts into the sea and fishermen still pull their boats up to a pebble beach backed by little houses. What to many visitors is Cefalù's greatest attraction stretches to the south of the old harbour – a long sandy beach that is one of the finest strands in Sicily.

Into the Madonie

South of Cefalù the **Madonie mountains** ❺ rise to an elevation of 2,000 metres (6,500ft), a wild landscape of woods, rocks and upland pastures. Unlike most of Sicily, the Madonie range has not been scarred by deforestation or urban blight. Every so often the winding roads come to the gates of a pretty hilltown.

Castelbuono, about 14km (9 miles) south of Cefalù on route 286, climbs the flanks of the enfolding hills, and its airy piazzas, usually backed by a church or two, afford some lovely views over the mountains. **Petralia Soprana**, 30km (19 miles) further into the mountains, is one of the most beautiful medieval towns in Sicily: it commands a hilltop, and stone palaces and churches line its medieval streets. Covered passageways lead to a belvedere with bracing views. **Polizzi Generosa**, 15km (9 miles) beyond, is at the head of a green valley and has 76 churches within its walls. The Chiesa Madre is the most opulent and is decorated with several sculptures

Thermal mud baths at Vulcano

by Domenico Gagini. It also has a 16th-century Flemish triptych and Venetian organ. The beautiful landscapes that stretch for miles around these towns are preserved as the **Parco Regionale delle Madonie** (www.parcodellemadonie.it) and can be traversed on a network of trails.

Tindari

Like so many Greek settlements in Sicily, **Tindari** ❻ is beautifully situated on a headland with sweeping views across the sea to the Aeolian Islands. This view can best be appreciated from the top of the **amphitheatre**. It was built by the Greeks but outfitted for gladiatorial spectacles by the Romans, who conquered the town in 254 BC, barely 150 years after it was founded.

A number of Roman houses also still stand, and several retain their colourful mosaic flooring. Tindari, which is about 120km (72 miles) east of Cefalù, is also famous for its **Madonna Nera** (Black Madonna), a Byzantine statue that is much venerated for its miraculous powers. The statue is housed in a huge church erected to accommodate the crowds that make a pilgrimage here, especially on 8 September, the Black Madonna's feast day.

Directly below Tindari and west of Oliveri lies one of Sicily's most entrancing beaches, forming part of the Riserva Naturale Laghetti di Marinello, where saltwater lagoons, sand dunes and dramatic rocky cliffs provide a sanctuary for migratory birds. The lagoons, fine sand and clean water are irresistible.

The Aeolian Islands (Isole Eolie)

This cluster of tiny volcanic islands off the northeast coast have long been popular with summer visitors, but are a delight off-season as well when they offer a real sense of adventure. The islands all have their own character, whether it's smouldering Vulcano, spectacular Stromboli or chic Panarea. The main island of Lípari makes an excellent base, and from here you can ferry hop to explore the smaller islands. If you prefer a smaller island, green, twin-peaked Salina is a wonderful choice, with excellent walking along waymarked mountain trails, and some fantastic places to eat and sleep.

Although the islands are small, quiet (off season at least) and best known for such simple pleasures as swimming, hiking, wine tasting and (in the case of Vulcano) soaking in mud baths, they played an important role in the affairs of the Mediterranean world. Ancient Greeks settled the islands and used them as a base for pirate raids, naming them after Aeolus, the hospitable God of the winds who lived on Lípari. Carthage launched attacks from them during the Punic Wars; the Romans prized their obsidian (volcanic

SICILY'S ACTIVE VOLCANOES

Mount Etna, the largest active volcano in Europe, distinguishes Sicily with its towering, smoking, drama. But like all volcanoes, its elevation varies according to its activity; it usually lies at about 3,323 metres (10,902ft). Curiously, while Stromboli rises to 924 metres (3,031ft) and Vulcano to 500 metres (1,640ft), these two island volcanoes are actually comparable in size to the great Etna. This is because their roots lie 2,000 metres (6,500ft) below sea level and only their summits are visible. In fact, Stromboli's active cone emerges directly from the sea.

glass that can be honed to a fine cutting edge); and marauders continued to invade well into the Middle Ages. The islands are most easily reached by boat and hydrofoil from Milazzo, a port 150km (90 miles) east of Cefalù.

Vulcano and Lípari

Vulcano ❼ is the island closest to the Sicilian mainland, though Lípari, just across the narrow Bocche di Vulcano, is the largest and the busiest. Vulcano's steaming volcano supplies the island with its most popular activities: soaking in *fanghi*, thermal mud baths that are said to cure skin disorders and arthritis, swimming in the sea above the warm bubbles of fumaroles, and hiking through a lunar landscape to view the crater that is the source of the sulphurous smell that hangs over the scruffy main town, Porto di Levante.

On **Lípari** ❽ the Museo Archeológico displays finds from the islands' long history, including tools and pottery left behind by Neolithic inhabitants – the museum is famous for its terracotta Greek theatre masks and figurines of dancers and actors, the world's largest such collection. Most visitors come to enjoy the island's beaches, many of which are covered in pumice and as a result are white, a curiosity in these parts.

Fontana di Orione, Messina

Other islands

Laid-back **Salina** ❾, a 25-minute boat hop from Lípari, is a lush and fertile island. The pretty village of Santa Marina di Salina is becoming increasingly chic, while the nearby hamlet of Lingua has a long traffic-free waterfront and a popular stony beach.

Though **Stromboli** ❿ is small and only sparsely inhabited, its ever-active volcano has ensured that it is the most famous of the islands. It has been in almost continual eruption and every 20 minutes or so, the volcanic crater hurls glowing multi-coloured chunks of lava into the sky and down a cliff called the **Sciara del Fuoco** ('stream of fire') into the sea, where they hiss and steam. You can witness this spectacle at close range from the rim of the crater; a guided ascent is one of the island's most popular activities and is most rewarding at night. For days when you just want to relax, there are long flat beaches, with volcanic black sand to the north of the jetty, stone and shingley sand to the south.

Among the other small islands, pretty **Panarea** ⓫ is where rich Italians and celebrities have summer homes, while sleepy **Filicudi** and **Alicudi** only come to life in the holiday season.

The Eastern Coast

Highlights

- **Messina**, see page 56
- **Taormina**, see page 57
- **Mount Etna**, see page 60
- **Catania**, see page 61
- **Inland to Enna and Piazza Armerina**, see page 64
- **Caltagirone**, see page 67
- **Siracusa (Syracuse)**, see page 67
- **Inland from Siracusa**, see page 74
- **Cava Grande del Fiume Cassibile**, see page 75
- **Val di Noto**, see page 75

Sicily's other large cities, Messina, Siracusa and Catania are on the eastern coast, and so is its most popular resort, Taormina. Remains of Roman and Greek settlements are copious, and many inland towns are built in the style of the Sicilian Baroque. Above all these places looms the fiery peak of Mount Etna, adding drama to the fascinating surroundings.

Messina

Messina ⓬, a busy port town 200km (124 miles) east of Cefalù, is where the eastern coast starts, leading south. It is within sight of mainland Italy, with Calabria across the Strait of Messina. This is often the first place where visitors set foot on Sicily; boats ferrying

The passeggiata at Taormina

cars and trains across the strait pull in and out of the harbour around the clock. The town's modern appearance and wide boulevards are the outcome of extensive rebuilding after earthquakes (the last one, in 1908, killed 85,000 residents – two-thirds of the population) and massive World War II bombings.

While most visitors hurry on to more atmospheric places, Messina rewards a short visit. The Duomo in the town centre is a felicitous and determined reconstruction of the church that Roger II erected in the 12th century. The 1908 earthquake levelled the church and it was rebuilt in the 1920s, and when a 1943 firebombing laid waste to these efforts, the city built the church once again. From the heights of the campanile comes a quarter-hourly chime accompanied by a theatrical show of revolving planets, goddesses and beasts; one of them, the town's symbolic lion, roars at noon. The 16th-century **Fontana di Orione** in front of the Duomo has miraculously escaped the ravages that have befallen Messina, and so has the simple, 12th-century church of the **Annunziata dei Catalani**.

Via Garibaldi and its continuation, Via della Libertà, lead north about 2km (1.5 miles) through the centre of town to its highlight, the **Museo Regionale**. This major collection has works by Antonello da Messina, Sicily's Renaissance master, including his *St Gregory* polyptych. Two of the most stunning works in the museum are by Caravaggio, the *Adoration of the Shepherds* and the *Resurrection of Lazarus*.

Taormina

Sicily's most famous and busiest resort clings to a hillside high above the sea and, is surrounded by luxurious tropical gardens that bloom year round, with Mount Etna as a backdrop. **Taormina** ⓭ is a small, medieval hilltown of pastel-coloured palaces, elaborate 19th century villas and a magnificent Greek Theatre are tucked away on narrow, often stepped streets. These charms are not

Teatro Greco, Taormina

current news. Taormina has been on the beaten track since the time of the aristocratic Grand Tourists, while D. H. Lawrence took such a shine to Taormina in the 1920s that he stayed three years. Taormina is popular with holiday-makers pretty much year round and seethes in mid-summer. The main activity is strolling the length of its pedestrianised, narrow main street, Corso Umberto, admiring the views of Etna and the bay, browsing its souvenir shops and visiting the cafés and restaurants.

Visitors arriving by taxi or bus enter the city at **Porta Messina**, the northern entrance that is a stroll from the *funivia* (cable car) that carries visitors up from the beaches below. The Corso starts here, lined with many 15th-century palazzi. One of them, the Palazzo Corvaja in the Piazza Vittorio Emanuelle, houses the tourist office, and this arrangement makes it possible to catch a glimpse of its ornamentation of black and white lava, the great hall where the Sicilian parliament met in 1410, and the elegant staircase in the courtyard.

The Teatro Greco and Giardino Pubblico

From Piazza Vittorio Emanuelle, the Via Teatro Greco leads to Taormina's beautiful **Greek Theatre** (http://teatrogrecotaormina.com, charge) . Though the Romans more or less rebuilt the structure, it is typically Greek in its splendid location, carved into the hillside in such a way that Mount Etna and the sea provide a permanent backdrop. As no less an observer than Goethe once exhaled into his diaries, 'Never did any audience, in any theatre, have before it such a spectacle.' The acoustics are excellent, and the theatre hosts a summer arts festival, Taormina Arte, which presents drama, cinema, ballet and music from June to October.

Via Bagnoli, Croce leads downhill off the Corso to the **Giardino Pubblico**, where stands of cypress and cedar frame idyllic sea views. From the very top of the town, a steep path climbs uphill to the ruins of the medieval *castello* and even higher to the little pretty mountaintop village of Castelmola perched on a limestone peak.

But stroll along the Corso. Enjoy the shopping or refreshments. The airy Piazza IX Aprile is filled with café tables and open on one side to views of the sea and Mount Etna. Through the **Torre dell'Orologio**, a 12th-century clock tower that straddles the Corso, you come to the Piazza del Duomo, where the crenellated, fortress-like **cathedral** backs a splashing fountain. Further on you come to Porta Catania, the town's exit.

GOLE DELL'ALCÁNTARA

Over the centuries the river Alcántara, fed by springs on Mount Etna, has cut a deep but enchanting canyon (www.parcoalcantara.it) into the basalt flow near Naxos (Taormina). Almost every strata of lava created by each volcanic eruption can be identified. The riverbed is reached on foot down the wooded hillside or by elevator, and in summer, when the waters are low, you can walk 150 metres/yds safely along the bumpy riverbed itself – to go any further than is permitted would lead to dangerous drops and waterfalls. The waters are cold but a visit is an exhilarating adventure and waders and wetsuits can be rented on site. Coaches depart from Taormina and Catania.

On the slope of Mount Etna

Mount Etna

Europe's largest and most active volcano soars 3,323 metres (10,902ft) above the Sicilian coast. Fiery **Mount Etna** ⓮ has long fascinated residents of Sicily and visitors to the island. Pindar and Pluto wrote about it, Empedocles died by jumping into its gaseous crater, and D. H. Lawrence and legions of other noted artists, intellectuals and writers have waxed poetic about one of Catania's most iconic symbols.

Sicilians keep a close eye on the volcano for good reason: molten lava flowed through Catania in 1669 and regularly plunges down the mountain towards the towns on its flanks. Eruptions occur on an almost annual basis, wreaking substantial damage on roads, houses and the tourism infrastructure on the flanks of the mountain. The volcano was particularly active in 2012, erupting dramatically several times during the year, and in 2017, 10 people were actually injured during an eruption. When the volcano is erupting, admirers are allowed to venture no further than Randazzo, Nicolosi and other towns and resorts in the green foothills; many can be reached on the **Circumetnea** railway, which leaves from Catania and skirts the mountain's lower flanks. Conditions permitting, **Rifugio Sapienza** is the base from which to make an ascent to the summit on foot or by the cable car (www.funiviaetna.com) and Jeep (see page 98).

Catania

Sicily's second largest city, 38km (24 miles) down the coast from Taormina, **Catania** ⓯ is grim and industrial in parts, but has a small, vibrant and recently restored **historic centre** of bold Baroque buildings, boisterous food markets and cutting-edge arts and entertainment.

Piazza del Duomo

This elegant, restored square lies at the southern end of the Via Etnea. The wide boulevard, Catania's main shopping street, makes a straight run through the city towards the looming, snow-capped volcano, only 20km (12 miles) away. The square and the **Duomo** are the work of Giovanni Battista Vaccarini, who came to Catania in 1730 to rebuild the city from the rubble to which it was reduced in a 1669 lava flow and a 1693 earthquake. Vaccarini's elegant assemblage surrounds the **Fontana dell'Elefante** (Elephant Fountain), crafted like most of Catania's monuments from black lava. Water cascades around a pachyderm with an Egyptian obelisk on its back, creating a pleasing effect that Napoleon copied in several of the monuments he commissioned in Paris.

Catania's cathedral

The **Duomo**'s medieval apses, built of lava, are all

that survived the earthquake, and they now lie behind a Baroque façade into which Vaccarini set several columns purloined from Catania's Roman ruins. Vincenzo Bellini, the composer of Norma and some of the other most popular operas of the early 19th-century, is buried in the church, as is Sant' Agata, the city's patron. Agata is a venerated presence in Catania, and has even influenced the city's famous pastries, *Cassatella di sant'Agata* – they are shaped like her breasts, which were cut off when she was martyred. (Catania honours Bellini with *spaghetti alla Norma*, named for his famous heroine.) To the right of the Duomo, the **Museo Diocesano** (https://museodiocesanocatania.com; charge) is home to the cathedral's collection of religious art and silverware,

Teatro Romano, Catania

but beautifully presented as the museum is, most people will find more appeal in the remains of the Terme Achilliane, Catania's **Imperial Roman baths**, which form part of the museum.

Catania's raucous fish, vegetable and fruit market fills the streets to the west of the piazza; to reach the warren of stalls, step through the Porta Uzeda. This lively commerce transpires in the shadows of **Castello Ursino**, the grim fortress from which Frederick II extended a firm hand over his Sicilian kingdom. Frederick built his castle on the seashore, but molten lava from the 1669 eruption landlocked the structure. The cavernous interior houses the eclectic holdings of the **Museo Civico**, restored and ranging from archaeological finds to Baroque statuary.

Piazza Mazzini and Via dei Crociferi

From the gardens in front of the castle it is a short walk up Via Auteri to Piazza Mazzini, surrounded by arcades crafted from 32 columns salvaged from a Roman basilica. More Roman remains rise just to the west: a remarkably intact theatre from the 2nd century BC and a small Odeon used for recitations and rehearsals. Vincenzo Bellini was born in the adjoining Piazza San Francisco, and the composer's house is now the **Museo Belliniano**, filled with his original scores and other memorabilia. A nearby house and museum, just off Corso Vittorio Emanuele on Via Santa Anna, commemorates another noted Catania native, the 19th-century novelist and short story writer Giovanni Verga. Although Verga is little read outside of Italy, his stark depictions of everyday life in Sicily have earned him the reputation as one of the great Italian masters of fiction.

Piazza San Francisco is at the foot of the **Via Crociferi**, with a succession of Baroque churches, convents and noble palazzi. **San Nicolò** to the west is the largest church in Sicily and certainly the most eerie. Work was curtailed by the 1693 earthquake and the church was later abandoned, incomplete. Restoration is currently

Fabulous mosaics at Villa Romana

underway. The huge adjoining Benedictine Monastery is now part of the university; guided visits reveal internal cloisters, a hanging garden and remains of a Roman house.

Teatro Romano

At the northern end of Via Crociferi, on busy Piazza Stesicoro, looms the hulking and recently restored **Teatro Romano**. Sant' Agata was thrown to the lions here in 252, before what may have been a sizeable audience – the vast amphitheatre seats 16,000 spectators. Looking up Via Etnea from the front of the theatre, it is easy to comprehend the power of a local legend that claims the citizens of Catania once stopped a lava flow from the nearby mountain by waving the saint's veil in front of it. If Etna is rumbling and spewing during your visit, you may well wish you were equipped with similar protection.

Inland to Enna and Piazza Armerina

Enna ⓰, 85km (52 miles) west of Catania on autostrada A 19, is the highest city in Sicily, lying about 900 metres (3,000ft) above a vast plain that once supplied the Greeks and Romans with wheat. This is not, however, Sicily's most cheerful city, surrounded as it often is by mist and huddled beneath a dark fortress erected by Frederick of Swabia in the 14th century.

On a clear day the views are splendid, and the best places to enjoy them are the central square, Piazza Crispi, or better yet, the Torre Pisana, one of six towers rising above the fortress. On the plains below, wheat fields stretch for miles across the centre of the island. Amid them glimmers **Lago di Pergusa**, the lake where Hades is said to have abducted Persephone, daughter of Zeus and goddess of fertility, and carried her off; the wheat died in Persephone's absence, but the earth bloomed anew when Hades released her. Today the lake is surrounded by a hectic motor race-track and fast food outlets.

Piazza Armerina

Most travellers pass through Piazza Armerina, on their way to the Roman villa, Villa Romana, at nearby Casale. The hill town, 35km (23 miles) south of Enna, warrants a short visit in its own right, too. The 17th-century Duomo tops the town, and from the piazza the streets wind down the hillside past churches and palaces to the palm-shaded Piazza Garibaldi.

Ceramics at Caltagirone

The Villa Romana at Casale

The **Villa Romana** ⓱ (www.villaromanadelcasale.it; charge) lies 5km (3 miles) southwest of Piazza

Teatro Greco in Siracusa

Armerina, outside the little hamlet of Casale. Co-emperor Maximian, who ruled the waning Roman Empire with Diocletian, is thought to have built this elaborate hunting lodge in the 4th century. Later, the villa was abandoned and eventually buried by landslides, and it wasn't completely unearthed until 1950. The many layers of mud that lay atop the ruins for centuries helped preserve the exquisite mosaics with which the villa is floored. Craftsmen from North Africa laid the colourful tiles, filling room after room with hunting scenes, a bestiary of exotic animals from the far corners of the empire, mythical heroes, chariot racing and snippets of everyday life, such as a family relaxing in the baths or groups of people fishing. The villa's most famous mosaic scenario is the one depicting ten girls, clad in bikinis, preparing to compete in a gymnastics competition.

Caltagirone

Citizens of the small town of **Caltagirone** ⓲, 35km (21 miles) southeast of Piazza Armerina, have been making ceramics for centuries. They show off their skill on every available surface: bridges, the 142 steps of La Scala (which climbs one of the town's three hills), the interiors of churches and the façades of houses are tiled with the town's distinctive blue-and-yellow ceramics.

Caltagirone would be attractive even without this adornment, since its old town is filled with Sicilian Baroque and Art Nouveau buildings; the church of **San Francesco d'Assisi** is an especially attractive example of the Sicilian Baroque. The **Museo della Ceramica** displays work from Caltagirone and elsewhere in Sicily, and the famous local product is for sale in workshops throughout the old town.

The Ear of Dionysius, a man-made cave

Siracusa (Syracuse)

What may well be Sicily's most enticing city is actually three places: the vast Greek and Roman city that played such a prominent role in the ancient world; the cultural island of Ortygia (now Ortigia), where the twisty narrow streets are lined with classical monuments and intricate Baroque churches; and a modern town of broad avenues and seaside promenades.

The greatest concentration of remains of ancient

EUREKA AND ARCHIMEDES

It is most unlikely Archimedes jumped from his bath crying Eureka! (Greek for 'I have found it!') on discovering the principle of specific gravity, even though physics teachers often say so. Born in Siracusa in 287 BC, the great genius and theoretician worked for Hieron, the Tyrant of Siracuse, and among his inventions for his country's war were a long-range catapult and a 4,000-ton ship with three decks, a gymnasium and garden. He was killed during the city's Roman occupation by a Roman soldier who failed to recognise the old man.

Siracusa is in the **Parco Archeológico della Neapolis** (http://aditusculture.com; charge) on the western edge of the modern city. Looking at these monuments, it is easy to appreciate the power Siracusa once wielded. Corinthians colonised Siracusa in the 8th century BC, settling on the island of Ortygia. Soon they set their eyes on the rest of Sicily and much of the Mediterranean world, defeating the Carthaginian and Etruscan fleets and eventually, in the so-called Great Expedition of 413 BC, the forces Athens sent to quell the ambitious Siracusans. Under such powerful and often tyrannical rulers as Hieron I and Dionysius the Elder, the city thrived and welcomed Pindar, Aeschylus, Plato and other great minds of the Hellenistic world.

The Romans, against whom Siracusa fought in the Second Punic War, finally subdued the city in 211 BC. Though Siracusa never again regained its power, natural harbours ensured the city would remain an important trading post. Early Christianity, bolstered by a visit from Saint Paul, flourished in Siracusa, and extensive catacombs beneath the city served as both tombs and churches.

The Parco Archeológico della Neapolis

Much of ancient Siracusa was built of limestone that slaves, captured in the city's numerous sea battles, dug out of quarries called the **Latomie**. Now overgrown with tropical foliage that lends a garden-like aspect to the archaeological park, the Latomie were also used as prisons. The cavern dubbed **Orecchio di Dionisio** **A**, Ear of Dionysius, seems to have been especially well suited to this purpose: legend has it the tyrant made use of the unusual acoustics, which allowed him to stand at the entrance and overhear anything a prisoner or guard within might whisper. The dampness of the adjoining **Grotta dei Cordari** provided ideal conditions for ropemakers, rendering the strands more pliant; the ropes fashioned here thousands of years ago have left deep indentations in the rocks.

Just beyond the Ear of Dionysius is the **Teatro Greco** **B**, one of the largest Greek theatres in the ancient world. Aeschylus wrote works to be performed on its stage. Of the original 59 rows of seats, 42 still remain and are filled during the summer months for popular performances of some of the ancient Greek dramas. The **Anfiteatro Romano** **C** served less refined tastes: built in the 3rd century AD, it staged circuses and gladiatorial events. Hieron II, who ruled all of Sicily from Siracusa throughout much of the 3rd century BC, commissioned his eponymous **Ara di**

The ruins of Greek fortifications on Ortigia, Siracusa

Siracusa Duomo

Ierone II **D**. The largest sacrificial altar in the Greek world was 200 metres (660ft) long and could accommodate 450 bulls at a time.

Basilica di San Giovanni and the Catacombs

Other remnants of ancient Siracusa are scattered about the city, often neglected and choked by weeds. A much-visited site is the city's oldest church, the **Basilica di San Giovanni** **E**, just north of Via Teocrito. Though the church has been a roofless ruin since the earthquake of 1693, it is possible to find the spot where Saint Paul delivered a sermon and the pillar to which Saint Marcian, the first bishop of Siracusa, was tied and flogged to death in 254. Steps descend to the **Catacombe di San Giovanni** **F**, (http://kairos-web.com; charge) part of a vast network of caverns that often follows the paths of subterranean Greek aqueducts. They provided a place of refuge for Christians during times of Roman persecution, and as Christian burial was forbidden under Roman law, so the passageways also served as tombs – it is believed that more than 20,000 early Christians are buried beneath San Giovanni.

The Museo Archeológico

Many of the finds from ancient Siracusa are displayed in the **Museo Archeológico Regionale Paolo Orsi** G (http://aditusculture.com) just south of San Giovanni on Via Teócrito. This is one of the most extensive archaeological collections in Europe and ranges far beyond Siracusa into the rest of the Mediterranean world. The prize of the collection, though, is from Siracusa: a headless Venus Anadiomene, modestly covering her nudity as she emerges from the water. Among the votive statuettes, burial urns and torsos, are tools and skeletons of the Stone and Bronze Age peoples who inhabited this corner of Sicily long before the Greeks arrived. Heading south to Ortigia, you could make a diversion to see Caravaggio's *Burial of St Lucy*, in the Basilica of Santa Lucia H (free).

Ortigia

A fist of land with the thumb downturned, ORTIGIA stuffs more than 2700 years of history into a space barely 1km long and 0.5km across, with ancient Greek temples, and Baroque churches and palaces caught in a tangle of streets (much of them following a medieval Arab street-plan). Its recent popularity has been accompanied by a wave of new bars, boutique hotels and restaurants. There is even a small beach.

Ortigia was connected to the mainland at different times by causeway or bridge: today the best approach on foot is from Corso Umberto I over a wide bridge to Piazza Pancali, where the sandstone remnants of the Tempio di Apollo sit in a little green park surrounded by railings. Today, Ortigia is one of the most popular tourist destinations in Sicily – as well

The **Tempio di Apollo** Ⓗ on sociable Piazza Pancali is a popular place to meet up before a night out. A few broken columns and marble fragments are all that remains of the structure, which dates from 565 BC and is thought to be the oldest Doric temple in Sicily. This temple was dedicated to Apollo, whose name is legible on the steps of the base. Corso Matteotti, lined with chain clothes and shoe shops, leads from the temple to Piazza Archimede, named for the Greek mathematician and inventor who was a 3rd-century BC resident of the city. Piazza Duomo, just south along the Via Roma, is perhaps the most spectacular square in Sicily, its gleaming limestone pavement overlooked by two elaborate churches and several theatrical palaces.

The **Duomo** Ⓘ captures Siracusa's long history, incorporating the entire body of a temple of Athena built in thanksgiving for a victory over the Carthaginians in the 6th century BC; you can see 12 columns from the temple embedded in the north wall. The church took on Byzantine elements when it became the first Christian cathedral of Siracusa in 640 AD, a Norman front that collapsed in the earthquake of 1693, and finally the dramatic, Baroque façade you see today, soaring above the

NOTES

Every summer, towards the end of June, the local council erects wooden swimming platforms on the rocks on the eastern coast of Ortigia, and at two points along the cycle path that runs along the coast from the Latomie dei Cappuccini. Access is free, and the platforms remain until the end of September – sometimes later. In Ortigia there is also a tiny beach at Cala Rossa; entrance by steps right below the Royal Maniace hotel. There are also smart lidos in Ortigia, one on the east coast (entry opposite the end of Via Maestranze), the other just below Fontana Arethusa. If you prefer a long, sandy beach, head to Arenella (a 40-minute ride on bus #23).

pavement cafes and street hawkers. The interior is quite sparse, but houses a number of statues by the Gagini, the illustrious clan of Baroque sculptors, and a fine painting of Saint Zosimus by Antonello da Messina.

Fonte Aretusa, Ortigia

Fonte Aretusa and Galleria Regionale

The western shore of Ortigia, just a few steps in front of Piazza Duomo, is the long seaside esplanade, the **Foro Italico**. This is where Siracusans come down from their apartments in the city for an evening *passeggiata*, accompanied by a view of the setting sun. Lord Nelson docked here, beside the **Fonte Aretusa** ❶, to take on fresh water en route to the Battle of the Nile. He drew from a renowned source: the fountain was famous throughout the ancient world as the metamorphosed nymph Arethusa. Fleeing the unwanted attentions of the river god Alpheius, she called on the goddess Artemis for help. Artemis turned her into a spring, and she flowed beneath the Mediterranean and emerged here – to no avail, since Alpheius followed her and forever mingles his waters with hers. The fountain continues to gush into a pool overgrown with papyrus. The promenade running south, the Lungomare Alfeo, is flanked by seaview restaurants and bars. At its end the **Castello Maniace** Ⓚ (www.aditusculture.com; charge) is a massive Swabian fortress that has been restored and is now open to the public.

View over the Baroque town of Noto

The Via Capodieci leads inland again to a handsome group of palaces. One of them, the 13th to 15th century **Palazzo Bellomo**, houses the **Galleria Regionale** ❶, (http://aditusculture.com; charge) the regional art gallery, highlight of which is Antonello da Messina's Annunciation.

Inland from Siracusa

The rocky plains and scrubby mountains that lie inland from Siracusa are littered with more ancient remains; it was here, too, that the Sicilian Baroque flowered in several small towns. On the plains 8km (5 miles) west of Siracusa, **Castello Eurialo** was the largest and most intricate fortification to survive from the ancient Greek world. Elaborate as the defences were, history would prove that they were built in vain – Siracusa eventually surrendered without a fight to the Roman legions. Enchanting **Palazzolo Acrèide**, 45km (28 miles) west of Siracusa, was an early colony of ancient Siracusa, founded as **Akrai** in the 7th century BC. It's hard to get a sense of Akrai's one-time glory in the clutter of its ruins, but the lovely, semicircular **Teatro Greco** is well preserved. Among the ruins are early Christian catacombs, a necropolis, stone carvings and votive niches. Don't neglect to explore the mazy streets of the old town, with decaying palazzi, theatrical Baroque churches, magnificent views and some very good pastry shops indeed.

Cava Grande del Fiume Cassibile

A spectacular winding route northwest of the ramshackle agricultural town of Avola climbs up to the magnificent gorge and nature reserve of the Cava Grande del Fiume Cassibile. There's parking by a sensational viewpoint over the Grand Canyon-esque Cassibile River gorge, with sheer rock walls visible across the divide, birds of prey circling and the river glistening far below. The very steep path that leads down to the valley bottom is closed at times of high fire risk, and an information booth posts warnings of the dangers of the descent – you certainly need to be properly shod, fit enough to climb back out, and to carry plenty of water. The round trip takes a good three hours, plus any time you spend swimming or sunbathing.

Val di Noto

The beautiful Baroque towns in southeastern Sicily, built after the terrible earthquake of 1693, were designed to

NOTES

Noto is Sicily's finest Baroque town, with all its principal buildings, palazzi and churches designed to be both theatrical and spectacular – which they are. Sicilians often dismiss it as a garden of stone, but as a UNESCO Heritage Site being restored to its former glory, the town centre's monumental pomp makes it a remarkable spectacle.

be blatantly theatrical and spectacular. Eight of the towns have been designated a World Heritage Site and their historic centres are seeing a revival with buildings restored to their former glory.

Noto

When an earthquake levelled **Noto** ⓳ on 11 January 1693, architects immediately set to work rebuilding the town. The Sicilian Baroque, a flamboyantly ornamental architectural style, was in full flower, and Noto was a blank canvas on which to show it off. Today this is the finest Baroque town in Sicily, drawing an ever-increasing number of tourists and day-trippers. The churches and palaces along the main street, Corso Vittorio Emanuele are fantasies of curving staircases, elaborate balconies, splendid porticos, and richly detailed façades. The grandest mansion is the restored **Palazzo Nicolaci di Villadorata**, with wonderfully ornate balconies and an elaborate interior with frescoed walls and ceilings.

Noto's cathedral

Riserva Naturale di Vendicari

A line of small-town resorts stretches south from Siracusa to Vittoria, with several sweeps of pristine sands in between – most notably at the Riserva Naturale di Vendicari (www.vendicari.net; charge), a lovely coastal nature reserve 10km south of Noto. Well maintained paths lead to unspoilt beaches of white-gold sand and salt lakes that, between October and March, attract flamingos, herons, cranes, black storks and pelicans. In the middle of the last century turtles disappeared from the area, perhaps thanks to the local appetite for turtle soup, but after careful management, they have now been encouraged back to Vendicari. At certain times, the local beaches are closed to allow them to breed in peace.

Ragusa

Ragusa ⓴, 50km (30 miles) west of Noto, is another Baroque town – at least half of one, since the older Baroque section, Ragusa Ibla, is separated from the newer, more ordinary Ragusa Superiore by a deep gorge (and a flight of 242 steps). The church of Santa Maria delle Scale (Saint Mary of the Steps) is a welcome spot to rest midway and enjoy a stunning view over the ochre-coloured town. Ragusa Ibla has been beautifully restored, and while nowhere near as busy as Noto, it is definitely on the tourist trail, and well known for its gourmet restaurants. At the highest point of Ragusa Ibla is the Piazza Duomo and Basilica di San Giorgio, the city centrepiece. Palm trees, a curving staircase leading up to the church and a façade of columns and balconies create a masterfully Baroque scene to accompany an evening drink or morning coffee.

Modica and Scicli

Perched on a ridge spilling down into a gorge the town of **Modica** ㉑ comprises the upper town (Modica Alta) and the lower town (Modica Bassa). Renowned for its chocolate, excellent shopping and gastronomy, it is a lively, thriving and unpretentious sort of place, which has so far managed to absorb tourism without being over-taken by it. The pride of Modica is the Baroque Duomo di San Giorgio perched precariously above the alleys of the historic upper town, surmounting a daunting Baroque flight of 250 steps.

Its rival is the opulent church of San Pietro, on the Corso, reached by another theatrical stairway.

Scicli ㉒, dramatically pitched against the bottom of a knobbly limestone bluff, is a gorgeous Baroque gem which is seeing a new lease of life. Palaces and churches have been skilfully restored, and in the wake of the town gaining fame from its starring role in the *Inspector Montalbano* TV series, restaurants, cafes, shops and chic places to stay have opened, although it still retains the authentic rhythms of a small Sicilian town. Via Mormino Penna is Scicli's showpiece, a scenographer's dream of a street, lined with exuberant and painstakingly restored Baroque churches and *palazzi*, including the Municipio fronted by the marvellous sculptural staircase that features in every episode of Montalbano as the location of the police HQ. Other highlights include the church of San Giovanni, which houses the astonishing Cristo di Burgos, a painting of Christ wearing what appears to be a white calf-length dirndl skirt (but is in fact a shroud).

The Southwestern Coast

Highlights

- **Agrigento**, see page 78
- **Selinunte**, see page 82

Two of the ancient world's greatest cities are next to the sea on the southern coast of Sicily, and Arab colonists have left their mark as well.

Agrigento

The poet Pindar described the city the Greeks knew as Akragas as the 'fairest of mortal cities'. You probably won't disagree with the sentiment as you look upon the dramatic vestiges of the ancient city, where a row of temples follows a ridge above the sea and a valley littered with ruins set among olive trees.

Unfortunately, the modern world intrudes upon this idyllic scene rather rudely. Modern buildings, constructed illegally, encroach upon the ruins. Workaday Agrigento, which occupies a hillside above the ancient city, is undistinguished, hastily put up in the 1960s after overbuilding triggered a catastrophic mudslide. What brings visitors to Agrigento are the ruins of the ancient city spread across the so-called Valle dei Templi (Valley of the Temples).

Valley of the Temples

In its heyday in the 5th century BC Agrigento rivalled Athens in splendour. Founded by settlers from Rhodes and Gela in 582 BC, it provided a good harbour and fertile soil and soon flourished – first under the tyrannical Phalaris, a member of a bull cult who allegedly burned his enemies alive in a bronze bull, then under Theron, who by the early 5th century BC had defeated the Carthaginians and extended the power of Akragas over much of the Mediterranean.

The city became known for its wealth and as a flourishing capital of 200,000 people who promoted the arts, philosophy and chariot racing. Empedocles, a native, developed the theory of the four elements (Earth, Air, Wind and Fire) and died when he dove into the crater of Mount Etna to

An afternoon in Scicli

investigate his premises. The philosopher had commented, 'The city's citizens enjoy life as they would die tomorrow, but they build palaces as if to live forever.' This prosperity, however, was short lived: Carthage sacked the city in 406 BC, and Rome invaded in 210 BC.

The arrival point of the **Valley of the Temples** ㉓ (http://coopculture.it; charge) is Piazzale dei Templi. The site is divided into two zones: Eastern and Western, linked by a walkway. Start with the Eastern zone, which has the main temples. The first and the oldest is the **Tempio di Ercole (Hercules)** Ⓐ, dating from the 6th century BC and now a romantic jumble of ruins from which nine of its original columns still emerge. A statue of Hercules and a fresco depicting the young god grappling with serpents once graced the temple, but these have long since vanished.

Follow Via Sacra to the superbly sited **Tempio della Concordia** Ⓑ. Built around 450 BC, this is the best-preserved temple at Agrigento (largely because it was converted to a Christian church in the 6th century), and one of the finest Doric temples of the ancient world. The stucco that once covered the temple has long since worn away, exposing warm, golden stone. At the end of Via Sacra stands the **Tempio di Giunone (Juno)** Ⓒ, which was built by the Greeks in 460 BC, and restored by the Romans after the handsome structure was destroyed by the Carthaginians; the stones are still scorched from the fires the invaders set. Earthquakes have also taken their toll, though a sacrificial altar and 25 of the 34 original columns have been set back in place.

In the Western Zone the stony remains of the **Tempio di Giove Olimpico (Jove)** Ⓓ are copious enough to suggest that this was indeed the largest Doric temple ever built. Enormous *telamones* (7-metre high columns fashioned in the shape of male figures) once supported the massive structure, and one of them, has been re-erected. West of the temple is a puzzling quarter dotted with pagan shrines. The Giardino della Kolymbetra (extra charge) is a large and fertile garden of citrus and other trees which has been restored and creates a delightful diversion from the temples.

Valley of the Temples

The Museo Archeologico and the Roman City

The **Museo Archeologico Regionale** ❺ (www.coopculture.it; charge) holds a wealth of artefacts excavated from the Valley of the Temples. Delicate vases, terracotta figurines, and an alabaster sarcophagus designed for a young boy and etched with scenes from his childhood provide an evocative glimpse into life in the ancient city. One room is dedicated to the Tempio di Giove Olimpico, with reconstructions of the temple and a reassembled *telamon*. Next to the museum spread the remains of the settlement that the Romans established when they took Agrigento permanently in 210 BC. Many of the houses they constructed on the Greek streets still stand, and their mosaic flooring is remarkably intact.

Modern Agrigento

The modern city also bears some traces of Agrigento's ancient inhabitants: **Santa Maria dei Greci** ❻, a small basilica rising above the stepped streets of the medieval quarter, is built of antique materials on the site of a temple to Athena; several columns are

The Temple of Venus in Segesta

imbedded in the walls of the church. **Santo Spirito** G is the church of a late 13th-century Cistercian convent whose nuns specialise in making almond and pistachio pastries (ring the doorbell marked 'monastero' next to the church to buy some). The church is rather dilapidated, but inside has fine Baroque stuccowork attributed to Giacomo Serpotta.

Luigi Pirandello, Agrigento's acclaimed 20th-century novelist and dramatist, was born in the seaside suburb of **Caos**. His birthplace, the **Casa Natale di Luigi Pirandello**, is now a museum, and his ashes are buried beneath a lone pine tree in the garden.

Selinunte

The city the ancient Greeks knew as Selunis (for the wild celery that still grows in abandon around the ruins) had little time to play an important role in the affairs of classical Sicily. Citizens were still building their city when Hannibal attacked in 409 BC; Selunis never recovered, and earthquakes have since levelled the remains.

Even so, **Selinunte** 24, 45km (27 miles) west of Sciacca, is one of the most evocative ancient sites in the Mediterranean, with ruined temples and monuments that now stand in lonely fields next to the sea. Three of the temples have been partially restored. They are designated by letter rather than name; to whom they were dedicated remains uncertain. **Temple E** is closest to the sea, and its massive columns have been set upright. The temple was possibly dedicated to Juno, wife of Zeus. **Temple G** was one of the largest Doric structures in Greek Sicily, though it was never completed; unfinished column blocks lie among its rubble. **Temple C**, which dates around mid-6th-century BC, stands at the highest point of the acropolis on the knoll of the hill and is the largest temple of all. The giant columns are nearly 2 metres (6.5ft) in diameter, except for those on the temple corners which are even thicker. It has provided the archaeological museum in Palermo with some of its greatest treasures – the metopes, or decorative friezes, that were once set atop its columns. A lengthy visit to the sprawling site can be followed by a swim along the sandy coast. The new settlement, **Marinella di Selinunte**, is a fishing port and resort, lined with lively restaurants.

The West Coast

Highlights

- **Mazara del Vallo**, see page 84
- **Marsala**, see page 84
- **Mozia**, see page 86
- **Trapani**, see page 87
- **Erice**, see page 88
- **Segesta**, see page 89
- **Capo San Vito**, see page 90
- **The Egadi Islands (Isole Egadi)**, see page 90
- **Pantelleria**, see page 91

Western Sicily was settled by Phoenicians, Greeks, Romans, Arabs, and the great European powers of the Middle Ages, and their presence is still much in evidence in the residential and ecclesiastical architecture.

Mazara del Vallo

Mazara del Vallo ㉕ may be of Phoenician origin but Arab influences predominate, from the Tunisian trawlermen to the Arab music and shisha hubble-bubble pipes. However, the Kasbah with its maze of backstreets has been newly gentrified with freshly painted houses and ceramic plaques and murals. The town has a long and pleasant tree-shaded seafront, with marina and beach, and a centre of fine churches. Within a deconsecrated church the **Museo del Satiro** (Satyr Museum) (charge) houses the 4th century BC bronze satyr, known as the Dancing Satyr. This was hauled up from the seabed by local fishermen and underwent a restoration in Rome. The statue is 2 metres (6.5ft) high and although both arms and a leg are missing you can see that the satyr is performing a wild ecstatic dance, his head thrown back and his hair flowing.

Marsala

The sleepy city of **Marsala** ㉖, 70km (43 miles) north and west of Selinunte, has a long and raucous past. The Phoenicians settled here in the 8th century BC, abandoned the city when they made the island of **Mozia** their stronghold, and came back when the Siracusans routed them in 397 BC. After a 10-year siege, the

MARSALA WINE

In 1773 English merchant John Woodhouse shipped 60 barrels of golden Marsala wine to England, adding a dose of alcohol to ensure it would survive the journey. The wine was an instant success and was soon stocked by the British navy, but Marsala later lost its reputation and was more or less relegated to cooking purposes. Recent years have seen a renaissance, with producers – no longer English – producing dry, smooth dessert wines, aged in oak barrels and known as Vergine or Riserva. The market leader is Florio (Via Vincenzo Florio 1, tel: 0923 78111), where you can taste various types of Marsala.

Romans took the city in 241 BC. Lilybaeum, as the city was then called, become the seat of the Roman governor of Sicily; by the time Caesar arrived on his way to Africa in 47 BC, Cicero had dubbed Lilybaeum a *civitas splendidissima*.

Marsala Cathedral

The port also proved to be a convenient gateway for the Arabs who overran Sicily in the 9th century; they called it 'the harbour of Allah', or *Marsa al Allah*. On 11 May 1860, the port of Marsala welcomed Garibaldi and the Thousand, the red-shirted freedom fighters who freed Sicily from Bourbon rule to unite Italy as a republic. Marsala bears its past glories with modesty. Of the ancient city, little remains but fragments of the Roman walls, some baths and a 3rd-century villa that's decorated with mosaics of hunting scenes and the four seasons. These are concentrated in the archaeological zone on the **Capo Boeo** promontory at the western edge of the city, which also happens to be the westernmost point in Sicily.

The nearby **Museo Archeologico** displays more Roman finds, including some colourful wall paintings and Phoenician ceramics. Most interesting, though, is a **Phoenician warship** that the Romans probably sank in the First Punic War. Discovered in 1971 on the seabed just north of Marsala, the boat is one of the few warships to survive from antiquity and has provided archaeologists with a wealth of information about the arts of ancient warfare.

The Old Town

The sweet, pleasant scent that pervades the city is that of an elixir that brought Marsala fame and fortune in the 18th century – Marsala wine (see box, page 84). British warships sent to protect England's interests in the Marsala business proved to be convenient for Garibaldi, who assumed they would also protect him when he made his landing here in 1860.

Garibaldi's presence in Marsala is commemorated by the Porta Garibaldi and the Via Garibaldi, which leads north from the port to the **Piazza della Repubblica**, the centre of town. The **Palazzo Comunale** and the **Duomo** face the square. Both have Baroque, 18th-century façades; sculptures by Antonello Gagini decorate the church.

Young Man in a Tunic, 5th-century BC statue at the Museo Whitaker

Mozia

The Phoenicians colonised the tiny island of San Pantelo in the 8th century BC and built **Mozia** ㉗, (www.isoladimozia.it; charge) one of their three cities on Sicily, set within a ring of ramparts and towers. They remained until Dionysius, the power-hungry Siracusan, routed them in 397 BC.

The Phoenicians went back and forth across the lagoon on a raised road, which now lay submerged beneath the shallow waters. Today's visitors reach the island by the ferry that departs from a landing stage opposite the island. The mainland near San Pantelo is marshy and parcelled into salt pans, and windmills that were once used to refine the salt rise above the flat landscape. One of the mills near the landing, the **Mulino Salina Infersa**, houses a small museum devoted to salt extraction.

Joseph Whitaker, from a prosperous family of Marsala wine exporters, bought the island and began to excavate the ruins in 1913. His finds lay scattered across the tiny, almost deserted island, and include the remains of the city walls, Punic dry dock (Cothon), a sacrificial site (Tophet), and a house with a floor of pebble mosaics. The **Museo Whitaker** (daily Apr–Oct 9.30am–6.30pm, rest of the year 9am–3pm) displays Punic and Greek finds from the island including the famous *Giovane in Tunica*, Young Man in a Tunic, an exquisite, 5th-century BC marble statue of a sinuous young man who may have been a charioteer.

Trapani

This city, 32km (19 miles) north of Marsala, has been a lively port town since Phoenician times and was once the centre of trade in coral, tuna and salt with the Levant, Carthage and Venice. Until recently it was seen as a workaday city in which to kill time before the next ferry to the islands. But **Trapani** ㉘ now has an elegant **historic centre** with restored churches and palaces, and a new seafront promenade. The old city is squeezed onto a narrow promontory that juts far into the sea, and the outskirts trail off into salt marshes where windmills catch Mediterranean breezes.

The sprawling modern outskirts are hardly welcoming but once in the old town it's well worth taking the time to stroll down the Corso Vittorio Emanuele to the **Torre di Ligny**, a restored squat Spanish fortress, built in 1671, at the end of the promontory. The street is lined with Baroque palaces and churches, and the sea poetically frames the end of the narrow side streets.

NOTES

Linking Trápani and Erice, the Funierice cable car (www.funiviaerice.it) takes just 12 minutes and affords wonderful views of saltpans, mountains, sea and islands.

Fom its port ferries sail to the Egadi Islands (see page 90) and Pantelleria (see page 91) as well as to Genova and Livorno, further away on mainland Italy.

Erice

Just 10km (6 miles) north-east of Trápani, **Erice** ㉙ is a world apart from that city or any place else in the modern world. Isolated on the heights of Monte Erice, the town has always enjoyed a lofty status. The ancient Elymians called the city Eryx and built a temple dedicated to Aphrodite (the Roman Venus), goddess of fertility. Aside from gathering fame throughout the Mediterranean world for its rich decoration, the temple served as a beacon for sailors navigating the trade routes to and from Africa. The Romans restored the temple several times; the Arabs considered the town holy enough to dub it *Gebel-Hamed*, Mohammed's Mountain; and the Norman Count Roger had visions of St Julian while besieging Erice and renamed it Monte San Giuliano. Even Mussolini saw the sanctity of the town and revived its ancient name.

The Normans built their **Castello di Venere** on the site of the ancient temple, taking advantage of the commanding position at the top of the town. Erice's public gardens now surround the castle, and from them rises the 15th-century **Torretta Pepoli**. Both castle and tower are ivy-covered, and the views from the garden terraces, over the plains and sea far below, are expansive – in fact, some keen-eyed observers claim to have seen all the way to Cap Bon in Tunisia.

The rest of the town is mostly medieval and clings precipitously to the shoulder of the summit. Battlements atop the tower of the stone **Chiesa Madre** are evidence of the double duty it did for the armies of Frederick III of Aragon, who used it as a lookout post; the interior of the church is surprisingly light and airy. Its campanile dates from 1315. At the heart of the city is its only square, Piazza Umberto I. Erice is a pleasant place to stop for a few days, and is within easy reach of most of the sights on the western and southern coasts.

Segesta

The Elymians, who lavished such attention on the temple in Erice (see page 88), settled **Segesta** ㉚ (www.parcodisegesta.com; charge) in the 12th century BC. By the 5th century BC, when Segesta's temple was built, the city had been heavily influenced by the Greeks who had colonised the island. It was busy warring with Selinunte, its neighbour on the southern coast.

The temple and a well-preserved theatre 4km (2.4 miles) away (with shuttle bus service) are the only sizeable remains of the ancient city, which is still being excavated. Their isolation, in green hills about 30km (18 miles) east of Trápani, lend the site a singular beauty. Both are among the finest monuments of antiquity, and both are set on hills looking over the rolling countryside and the sea.

Greek theatre at Segesta

Capo San Vito

This mountainous cape at the northwestern tip of Sicily, 40km (25 miles) north of Trápani, has the finest beaches on the island around the resort of **San Vito lo Capo** ㉛ and rugged headlands that are ideal for hiking. The **Riserva Naturale dello Zingaro** ㉜, a beautiful nature preserve just to the southeast, paths follow 6km (4 miles) of forested coastline, home to falcons and buzzards and etched with lovely coves, is thankfully recovering well after a devastating wild fire in 2020.

The Egadi Islands (Isole Egadi)

Trápani is the jumping-off point for the three **Egadi Islands** ㉝ in this sparsely populated archipelago. The nearest and largest island, Favignana, is only 25 minutes away by hydrofoil.

The crystalline waters are a paradise for swimmers and scuba divers and all of the islands offer good walks across unspoiled landscapes. **Favignana** is the most populated, though only 4,400 people live on the island and the number has decreased with the decline of the late-spring *La Mattanza*, the great tuna massacre which would see fishermen net and harpoon hundreds of tuna at a time. However, the recent restoration of the Tonnara di Favignana, a former tuna cannery and now a tuna heritage museum, has given the island hope of attracting more visitors.

On barren **Levanzo**, prehistoric inhabitants of the cave now known as the **Grotta del Genovese** left behind Neolithic paintings and Paleolithic carved drawings, mostly of animals. You can reach the caves by boat from the port in Levanzo town, or walk to them along the island's only road and a dirt path; both routes provide views of the **Faraglione**, a rocky spire erupting from the sea.

Marettimo is the most isolated of the islands, and unlike Favignana and Levanzo, is mountainous and verdant. Any resemblance this lovely landscape bears to those described in ancient mythology may not be coincidental: it's been long suggested that

Marettimo is in fact Ithaca, featured in the epic poem *Odyssey*, the home which Odysseus yearned to return.

Pantelleria

This windswept island of **Pantelleria** ❸❹ is closer to North Africa than it is to the rest of Sicily, 110km (66 miles) from Trápani and 70km (42 miles) from Tunisia. Pantelleria can be reached by plane or boat from Trápani and by plane from Palermo. The island also provides the opportunity to experience an unusual climatic phenomenon, a constant breeze that gives Pantelleria its name, from the Arabic *bint-al-rian*.

Levanzo town, Egadi Islands

A good network of buses provides transport to most spots of interest, including the island's few manmade attractions. These include remnants of prehistoric settlers of which the most fascinating is **Sesi**, a collection of funeral mounds on the southwest coast in which black volcanic rock is piled into high mounds. More in evidence are the island's distinctive traditional white-washed *dammusi* houses, first introduced by Arab colonists.

Similarly exotic is the island's black soil, the legacy of its volcanic peak. The volcanic presence also accounts for the hot springs that bubble up around the island. Some of the most appealing are at **Scauri**, not far from Sesi, where you can soak in warm natural pools and then jump into the sea.

Ballarò market, Palermo

Things to do

Aside from the extensive historical sites and sights, Sicily provides a host of other diversions. Many of these activities allow you to enjoy the island's beautiful landscapes of seacoasts and mountains.

Shopping

Although Sicily now has its first designer mall (see page 94), shopping on the island is not so much about Gucci or Armani as atmospheric street markets, ceramic workshops, black-lava souvenirs and gastronomy. The best shopping is in Palermo, Catania and Taormina. In Palermo, most of the better shops are concentrated around Piazza Verdi and Via della Libertà. In Taormina, the Corso Umberto is lined with shops, including palatial boutiques belonging to Dior and Dolce and Gabbana. Catania's Via Etnea, especially between Piazza Stesicoro and Piazza del Duomo, is the main shopping precinct. There are food and drink temptations wherever you go: chocolate from Modica, pistachios from Bronte, pastries from everywhere and dessert wines (Moscato and Malvasia) from the Aeolian islands and Pantelleria.

Antiques. Some of the most distinctive items to show up in antiques shops are pieces of the painted carts *(carretti siciliani)* that were once the mainstay of transport in the countryside. You can occasionally find plaques of wood from the carts covered in bright designs in the antiques shops of Palermo, Erice and Taormina. Another place to look for them is among the stalls of the daily flea market behind the cathedral in Palermo.

Ceramics. The town of Caltagirone, southwest of Catania, has been producing ceramics for centuries – even the 142 steps of its monumental staircase are covered in colourful tiles of local manufacture. Workshops around the town continue to make and sell tiles and other ceramics goods. Santo Stefano di Camastra, on the northern coast, also makes excellent ceramics.

Coloured ceramic vases from Caltagirone

Crafts. Erice is known for its hand-loomed cotton rugs, and they are available in several shops in town. In Taormina, several shops sell embroidered linens. Several local markets sell hand-woven baskets, and occasionally you will find a basket weaver demonstrating their art in a shop or market stall.

Fashion. Sicilia Outlet Village (www.siciliaoutletvillage.it) on the Autostrada, just east of Enna, is Sicily's first luxury designer shopping mall where fashions are discounted by 30–70 percent. For fashion elsewhere head to the boutiques of Taormina, Palermo or Catania where you can find designer clothes from many big-name Italian designers.

Souvenirs. Aside from the glowing replicas of Mount Etna and all manner of items made from black lava, look for the delightful replicas of the puppets that are the stars of Sicily's popular puppet theatres. The Museo Internazionale delle Marionette in Palermo (see page 44) can direct you to craftspeople who make the most authentic replicas of the puppets.

Weekly markets

Sicilian street markets provide most of the staples of life, and vendors sell clothing, household items, hardware, appliances and an enormous variety of food, including fresh fruit, vegetables, seafood, meat and cheese. In the main cities you'll also come upon stalls selling street food, and in the large, daily markets in bigger cities there are usually several excellent restaurants. Any town of any size in Sicily has a market at least one day a week, usually in the morning.

In Palermo, the two largest markets in the centre of the city are the Ballarò, around Piazza Carmine in the Albergheria quarter (see page 36); and the Capo. Both are held daily except Sunday. There is also a daily flea market in the streets behind the cathedral. In Catania, the market fills the streets between Piazza Duomo and Castello Ursino.

Sports and outdoor activities

Sicily has increasing appeal for active visitors. Coasts, islands and mountains lend themselves to year-round sporting activities. You can hike in hills and mountains, explore the underwater sea world and shipwrecks, quad bike on Etna, wade through gorges and explore offshore islands.

Cycling. Typical bike tours, offered by agencies, include Etna, the Val di Noto, the Marsala coast or the offshore islands, where cycling is particularly popular and reflects the slower pace of life. Most of the islands have mountain bikes (and often e-bikes as well) to rent at the port.

Hiking. Sicily's rugged terrain is well suited to hiking, though there are relatively few established trail networks. An exception is the

Madonie mountains, where marked trails ascend the peak of Pizzo Carbonara (1,979 metres/6,495ft) and crisscross the wooded terrain beneath them. For information see www.parcodellemadonie.it. The Riserva Naturale dello Zingaro (www.riservazingaro.it) protects the coast just east of Capo San Vito, and its trails follow the sea – from them you can scramble down to secluded coves – and cut through forest-covered mountainsides. The volcanic landscapes of Etna exert an obvious pull for hikers, but it is advisable to take a guide. The Aeolian and Egadi islands offer excellent opportunities for hiking, from climbing the craters of Vulcano and Stromboli to off-the-beaten track exploration of remote Filicudi or Marέttimo. For the ascent of Stromboli, a guide is compulsory.

Hikers on Vulcano in the Aeolian Islands

Scuba diving, watersports and snorkelling. The waters off Ustica, a tiny island 60km (36 miles) north of Palermo, provide the best locale for both activities. A stretch of the coastline is designated as a natural marine reserve, and equipment rentals and PADI certified dive schools are plentiful. The Aeolian islands are also a good destination for divers. (see page 139) An ever increasing number of water sports outfits on beaches rent out SUPs and sea-kayaks.

Sailing. The main ports for chartering sailing boats, with or without a professional crew are Marina di Ragusa, Giarre and, for exploring the Aeolian Islands, Porto Rosa on the Tyrrhenian coast.

Skiing. While Sicily will never be an internationally renowned ski resort, its higher peaks have lifts and other facilities. The ski resorts on Etna are Linguaglossa on the northern side and Nicolosi on the southern side. In the Madonie mountains, the main ski resort is the alpine village of Piano Battaglia.

The beach at Cefalù

Swimming. The beaches at Sicily's famous seaside resorts of Cefalù and Taormina are adequate but crowded, and the same can be said of Mondello, the seaside getaway for Palermo. Sicilians, like most Italians, like comfort on their beaches, and throughout the summer lidos are set up, where you can rent sun loungers and umbrellas by the day or week (or even month). They always have loos, and usually a bar and restaurant as well. You'll find more isolation on the long sandy beaches of Sampieri, near Scicli, and either side of the Vendicari nature reserve. Some of the most enjoyable swimming is from the beaches on the islands off Sicily – especially Maréttimo in the Egadi Islands and the less-crowded of the Aeolians. There are many beaches that do not appear on maps – just look out for little side roads (some of them un-surfaced) whenever you are driving along a coast road, as they will almost inevitably lead to a local beach. As jellyfish are common it is wise to wear a mask and snorkel – at least to check the water before you dive in.

Volcano viewing. Sicily has two of the few active volcanoes in Europe, Mount Etna on the island's eastern coast and Stromboli in the Aeolian Islands. Conditions permitting, you can begin an ascent to the crater area on Etna from Rifugio Sapienza on foot or by cable car to the Rifugio Montagnola, from where you can continue on foot or in a Jeep. Tour agencies and several hotels offer full day excursions to Mount Etna from Taormina – the best are led by a qualified volcanologist.

The volcano on Stromboli puts on an around-the-clock performance: every 20 minutes or so, the crater hurls glowing multicoloured chunks of lava into the sky, down a cliff (called the Sciara del Fuoco) and into the sea, where they hiss and steam. You can witness this spectacle independently (unless conditions are particularly dangerous) from a viewpoint that is a safe distance from the activity and reached by a well-marked path; if you want to get closer to the action a guide is obligatory. The best treks are timed so that you reach the summit at sunset, watch the eruptions as night falls, and then descend in the dark. You can also view the spectacle on private boat trips from the island's tiny port, from Lipari and Salina. The best trips will let you see the eruptions at night, and often serve a simple dinner of pasta with freshly caught fish.

Nightlife

Sicilians, like all Italians, love the evenings, and except on the coldest and rainiest night in the middle of winter, the main street or piazza of every town and village, will be full of people strolling, chatting, window-shopping, eating ice cream or sitting over an Aperol or Campari spritz in pavement cafes. Everyone dresses up, and the evening *passeggiata* (stroll), as it is known, is one of the most enjoyable aspects of daily life on the island and not to be

Palermo's Teatro Massimo

missed. Larger towns will inevitably have a couple of bars that are aimed solely at the night crowd, but only Palermo, Taormina and Catania have truly vibrant night scenes. Taormina's in summer is the most flamboyant, with a thriving LGBTQ+ scene. In summer on beaches around the island, many of the lidos turn into clubs at night.

Culture

Some of the most memorable performances in Sicily are the seasonal events held in the island's Greek theatres. Between May and June different dramatic cycles are performed in amphi-theatres from Siracusa and Segesta to Selinunte, Agrigento and Morgantina. In **Taormina**, the Greco-Roman theatre draws visitors from around the world for its annual music and opera festivals. The

International Greek Theatre Festival (www.indafondazione.org) is held every year at the Greek theatre in **Siracusa**.

Palermo offers a great season of opera, ballet and concerts at the Teatro Massimo (www.teatromassimo.it) in Piazza Verdi, and other concerts are performed in churches around the city. Classical and jazz concerts are held in the cloisters and roofless church of Lo Spasimo, an evocative entertainment complex set in a former 16th-century monastery in the La Kalsa quarter.

Teatro Massimo Bellini in **Catania**, named after the composer Vincenzo Bellini, is a world-famous venue for operas and concerts from October through May, and throughout the summer the city's Baroque churches and an outdoor stage in Piazza Bellini are the settings for concerts of classical and popular music. Catania is cooler for a young crowd than Palermo, with its late-night bars, live music venues, jazz and blues. As an energetic university city it offers events ranging from pop-rock spectaculars to open-air summer festivals. Zò (www.zoculture.it) is the futuristic culture and arts centre, housed in an ex-sulphur refinery.

Erice's churches and other venues open their doors for performances of medieval and Renaissance music throughout the summer; **Noto** hosts concerts from January to June while its Baroque churches and convents are the venues for the International Music Festival Notomusica in July and August; and the glittering, mosaic-filled cathedral in **Monreale** is the setting for a festival of ecclesiastic music during the first week of November.

Puppet Theatre

This lively entertainment, with its elaborate costumes, non-stop action and touches of humour, has been delighting Sicilian children and adults for centuries. Even audiences who don't speak Italian and aren't familiar with the tales, which are usually based on exploits of knights in the court of Charlemagne, find this spectacle engrossing. In Palermo, the Museo Internazionale delle Marionette

Puppet theatre

regularly stages performances. Palermo's Teatro di Via Bara (www.figlidartecuticchio.com) presents reinterpreted versions of traditional puppet theatre. Plays featuring puppets can also be seen in Acireale, Catania and Siracusa.

A puppet show is usually part of the festivities at fairs and other public celebrations in Sicily. Travelling troops tour the island in the summer months, often making stops in the resorts. Local tourist offices can let you know where and when you can find performances.

Cooking classes

There are scores of ordinary Sicilian people offering cooking classes, followed by cooking lunch in their home, but quality varies wildly, so be sure to check reviews carefully before signing up. Far better to opt for an experienced professional. In Palermo, Duchess Nicoletta Polo Lanza Tomasi's cooking experience starts with a fascinating tour of a market, where you'll learn about Palermo's history as well as its food, followed by cooking lunch in her family's palazzo (www.butera28.it/it/lezioni-cucina-siciliana-palermo/). For anyone seriously interested in Sicilian cuisine, cooking courses at the prestigious Anna Tasca Lanza cooking school (https://annatascalanza.com) cannot be beaten.

Children's Sicily

Sicilians shower attention on their children, and will probably do the same with yours. Welcome as children are in museums,

Traditional painted cart

restaurants and just about any other place in Sicily, you may want to seek out some activities that will provide a break from trudging through ruins and archaeological museums. Some suggestions:

Cefalù and **Taormina** are pleasant to visit with children, because the low-key, car-free old town centres provide plenty of diversions (especially the Greek theatre and views of Mount Etna in Taormina), and both beaches and countryside are nearby. **Erice**, ideally reached by the panoramic cable car from Trapani, is also a good place for young travellers to unwind, and they can wander the medieval streets, explore the ruined castle and enjoy the stunning views.

In **Palermo** a walk through the Ballarò or Capo markets will provide plenty of diversions, as will a stroll along the rebuilt Foro Italico, the new seafront. The Arab and Norman sights, with their whiff of exoticism, may be popular – especially the cathedral in Monreale, with its mosaics and cloisters, and the church of San Giovanni degli Eremiti, with its gardens.

Of the classical sights, **Selinunte** is probably the most child-friendly, because of the lack of crowds and its nearby beaches and adjoining fishing port. With their volcanic peaks, black sand beaches and blue waters, the **Aeolian Islands** might appear like a magic kingdom to youngsters (after all, this archipelago has inspired many a myth) and the trip from island to island on ferry can be fun. **Stromboli**, with its ever-active volcano, is always fascinating to view and sure to please. Of course, an ascent up **Mount Etna** is mandatory; a trip around its lower flanks on the Circumetnea railway may be the best approach if the young ones aren't up to arduous treks across the lava, or there are donkey rides too (Etna Donkey Trekking; https://experience.etnadonkeytrekking.it). The Roman mosaics at **Casale** will enchant even a sight-weary child.

Parents with very young children in tow may want to avoid the treasuries of churches, which are often filled with withered extremities and other ghoulish relics. A visit to **Palermo**'s Catacombe del Convento dei Cappuccini, where thousands of preserved corpses

Floats during Carnevale in Acireale

are draped about the premises, may or may not be appropriate, depending on a child's age and sensitivities. The catacombs in **Siracusa**, meanwhile, are corpse-less but spooky and atmospheric nonetheless.

Children will no doubt be delighted to visit Etnaland aquapark in **Belpasso**, the biggest amusement park in southern Italy (www.etnaland.eu) or Monti Rossi Adventure Park in **Nicolosi**.

Festivals and events

Sicilians celebrate festivals year-round. The following are just a few of the many events held throughout the island.

6 January In Piana degli Albanesi outside of Palermo, costumed citizens join a procession to celebrate Epiphany.

February–March Many towns celebrate Carnevale, most notably Sciacca (on the west coast), Cefalù, Taormina, and Acireale, north of Catania.

Holy Week Erice, Noto, Enna, Trapani, Marsala, and many other towns note this solemn religious period with special observations; however, in San Fratello, in the hills above Cefalù, citizens celebrate the Festa dei Giudei (Feast of the Jews) by donning costumes and parading through the streets on Maundy Thursday and Good Friday.

May Madonna delle Milizie in Scicli, in which a battle between the Normans and Arabs is re-enacted.

Mid-May–June Siracusa's Teatro Antico hosts a festival of ancient Greek theatre.

10–15 July All of Palermo takes to the streets for a boisterous festival in honour of Santa Rosalia, the city's patron.

July Taormina's Film Festival, held in the ancient Greek theatre, may not be Cannes, but it does attract a fair number of celebs.

First week of August Siracusa hosts its *palio*, in which boats manned by crews from the town's five quarters race around Ortigia island.

15 August (Ferragosto) The zenith of summer fun. Fireworks in pretty much every town and village on the island. The resort of Capo d'Orlando, east of Cefalù, celebrates the Feast of the Assumption with a procession of boats.

24 August The island of Lipari celebrates the feast of San Bartolomeo with fireworks and a procession around a statue of the saint.

8 September The sanctuary of the Black Madonna in Tindari is a pilgrimage destination.

September–October Taormina International Music and Opera Festival at the Greek theatre.

December Opera season begins in Palermo. Taormina celebrates the Christmas season with concerts and puppet shows and kicks off the New Year with a spectacular fireworks display.

13 December Siracusans carry a silver statue of their patron, Santa Lucia, through the streets to commemorate her feast.

Food and drink

Eating in Italy is good, but eating in Sicily is even better, an experience you will never forget, and that may have you packing your suitcase with the wild oregano, fruity chilli flakes, umami-rich tomato extract and toasted almonds that make Sicilian cuisine unique. Eating in Sicily means quite literally eating the island's history, as every one of its invaders left its mark on the food as well as the architecture. The ancient Greeks were already dab-hands at trapping tuna and making ricotta, and the Romans planted the island with vast wheat fields, but it was the Arabs who changed everything, introducing irrigation techniques perfected in the deserts of North Africa. Pistachios, sugar cane, rice, saffron, lemons, peaches, nectarines, mangos, melons were all grown. The Spanish introduced the tomatoes their conquistadores had discovered in South America, and imported cocoa beans. Today's cuisine is based on the vegetables that grow year-round, fish, especially *tonno* (tuna) and *pesce spada* (swordfish), and local olive oil, cooked with ingredients such as capers, raisins, wild fennel, almonds, pistachios and saffron that are the legacy of the island's Arab heritage. You will even find couscous on menus in the south and west of Sicily.

WHAT TO EAT

Antipasto means 'before the meal', and these are usually cold and in small portions. A selection of grilled vegetables, marinated anchovies, or local cheeses and salamis are typical.

Il Primo is the first course, and in Sicily that generally means pasta, which is often made with fresh seafood. The two signature Sicilian *primi* are *pasta con le sarde*, with fresh sardines, raisins, wild fennel and pine nuts and *spaghetti alla Norma* with tomato, basil, fried aubergine and ricotta cheese.

Il Secondo is the main dish, which in Sicily is often fish, though chicken, veal, lamb and pork also appear on menus.

Contorni are vegetables, almost always ordered separately.

Meat, especially beef from the Ragusa area and pork from the Nebrodi mountains, tends to be more popular inland, though you will often find rich beef and lamb ragù accompanying pasta dishes. Pasta sauces too are often made with vegetables and perhaps the island's best-known culinary contribution is *Spaghetti alla Norma*, named for the heroine of the opera by native son Vincenzo Bellini and made with fried eggplant (aubergines), tomatoes and salted. Sicilian desserts are very sweet – the most famous are cassata featuring sweetened ricotta, marzipan and candied fruit, and cannoli, crunchy deep-fried wafer tubes filled with sweetened ricotta and decorated with candied orange peel, chocolate or pistachio (and sometimes all three).

Crispy arancino

Top ten things to try

1. Arancino

Italian for 'little orange,' these oval-shaped deep-fried rice balls coated in breadcrumbs are traditionally filled with either *ragù* and peas or ham and cheese. In the most inventive places, you will find wonderful combinations such as sausage and mushroom, aubergine, tomato and ricotta, or cheese and vegetables.

2. Granita

Try a Sicilian flavour such as mulberry or pistachio, and look out for granita made with fresh Sicilian mango and ricotta granita scattered with candied capers, mint and a sprinkle of caper salt.

3. Sicilian avocados

These avocados from Mount Etna are best served in Sicilian salads with sundried tomatoes and burrata cheese. They are often described as having a more nutty and buttery taste than other more common avocado varieties.

4. Pasta alla Norma

The Sicilian classic, named after the heroine in the opera by native son Bellini, has a rich tomato sauce full of golden-fried aubergine, grated *ricotta salata* (salted ricotta) and fresh basil leaves. It's usually served with penne pasta.

5. Cassata

Quintessential Sicilian excess – a sponge base, and a mound of sweet ricotta wrapped in pistachio marzipan decorated with icing and candied fruit.

DOLCI (DESSERTS)

The Arab inheritance is reflected in watermelon and jasmine jellies, sorbets and *cassata siciliana*, and the cloyingly sweet sponge cake with almond paste and candied peel. The classic island favourites are cannoli, fried pastry tubes filled with ricotta, candied fruit, and *frutti alla Martorana* (fruit-shaped almond paste). *Crespelle di riso* are pancakes made with sweetened rice. Fruit, ricotta, honey, almonds and pistachio nuts often flavour cakes, ice cream and sorbets. Ice cream is often served inside a sweet brioche roll, and a popular sweet treat is *granita con brioche* (ice-cold fruit or coffee granita and brioche buns), which is eaten for breakfast rather than for dessert.

Pistachio gelato, almond and chocolate granita and freshly baked brioches

6. Cannoli

Look out for places that fill cannoli as you wait. These deep-fried wafer cubes are filled with sweetened ricotta and decorated with chocolate, candied orange peel, or pistachio (sometimes all three).

7. Swordfish involtini

Thin slices of swordfish are wrapped around an herb and garlic filling. Sometimes, pine nuts and raisins are added. The fish can be oven-baked or grilled on skewers over hot coals.

8. Pasta con le sarde

A Sicilian signature primi, *pasta con le sarde*, with fresh sardines, raisins, wild fennel, and pine nuts, is said to have been the first dish the Arab invaders cooked themselves upon landing in Sicily.

Chocolate from Modica

9. Modica chocolate

Try the special chocolate with a grainy texture made using a technique learned from the Azteks by Spanish conquistadores. Mainly made with just cocoa and sugar, it has no added fats, giving it a uniquely sweet and bitter note. There are plenty of chocolate boutiques in Modica, and Antica Dolceria Bonajuto (Corso Umberto I, www.bonajuto.it) is one of the best. Here, you can try different variations and learn more about the process.

10. Avola Rum

Sugar cane plantations once existed all over Sicily. The tradition continues in Avola, between Noto and Siracusa, where the sugar syrup is turned into rum using traditional methods. Best served neat or on the rocks.

Where to eat

Restaurants are usually referred to as *trattoria* or *ristorante*, and though the terms have come to denote establishments of similar character, in principal at least they are quite different. A trattoria is casual, serving home-style fare in an informal setting; a ristorante implies smarter décor, more polished service and more elaborate, more expensive cuisine. You will also find *osterias* – traditionally a simple inn -- but these days the term is used by upscale eateries who want to convey that their cuisine is based on simple, fresh and seasonal produce. Pizzerias are everywhere – look out for places using ancient Sicilian wheat varieties, sourdough starters (*lievito madre*) and long fermentation techniques.

Bars in Sicily and elsewhere in Italy are not just places to drink alcoholic beverages. They sell wine and spirits, as well as soft drinks, mineral water and coffee. They also serve light fare: pastries *(cornetti* or *brioche)* croissants filled with jam, custard, or chocolate in the morning. Savoury pastries will be on sale all day, usually displayed on the counter, you need only point to what you want.

Many Sicilians will stop by their local bar several times a day for a quick coffee and chat, and you should find one you like and do the same – there's almost no better place in which to observe the engaging drama of day-to-day Sicilian life.

Sicily has a long tradition of street food, especially in Palermo and Catania. Look out for chickpea fritters (*pannelle*), potato croquettes with anchovy and *caciocavallo* cheese (*crocche di patate*), and – for adventurous offal-lovers – beef spleen or tripe roll (*pani cu'la meusa*). Sicilian street food is these days often sold from tiny take-aways but you will still find itinerant stalls in the markets of Palermo and Catania.

A *caffè* and its kindred *pasticcerie* usually serve pastries and other sweets (often ice cream, or *gelato*) and sometimes light meals, accompanied by coffee, tea, or a glass of wine. An establishment or two like this grace the main piazzas of most towns in Sicily.

Pasta alla Norma

One more essential stop when travelling in Sicily is a *gelateria,* a shop that sells *gelato* (ice cream) and the Sicilian speciality, granita, a water-based ice made with fresh fruits or nuts, which was introduced to the island under Arab rule. Try mulberry *(gelsi)*, pistachio, peach *(pesca)* or watermelon *(anguria)*.

What to drink

Sicilians never drink tap water, and nor should you, because water is often stored below houses in cisterns, that may not have been regularly cleaned. Instead, drink mineral water *(acqua minerale). Acqua frissante, con gas,* or *gassata* all mean sparkling mineral water, *acqua naturale* or *non gassata* is still.

While international canned soft drinks are ubiquitous, there are some interesting Sicilian brands too, such as Polara, where the flavours range from pomegranate to green mandarin. *Spremuta* is a fresh-squeezed juice, made with oranges *(arance)* or lemons *(limone)* grown on the island and a sure-fire remedy for the effects of the sweltering summer heat; if you order a *spremuta di limone,* you will want to add sugar and water to your taste – Sicilians will often add salt.

Italian beer is excellent; ask for a *birra nazionale* and you will probably be served a bottle of Peroni or a Messina, which is brewed in Sicily, but there are an increasing number of craft breweries. Many imported brands are also available, especially Kronenbourg and Heineken. Draft beer *(birra alla spina)* is often imported and more expensive than you might expect.

Spirits are widely available, and are served neat, without ice, unless you ask for it *(ghiaccio)*. It is customary for the bar to give you a complimentary selection of bite-size savouries with them. The island also makes several rather sticky and bitter, herbal tasting liqueurs, including Averna, which is made in Caltanissetta, and Fichera, from

FRUTTI ALLA MARTORANA

Sicily is famed for its local produce and, at every social level, Sicilians enjoy good food and wine, often the simpler, the better. As anyone who has visited a *caffè* or *pasticceria* (confectioner) will have noticed, sweet decorated desserts, cakes and ice creams are particular favourites. There is an abundance of confections made with almonds too – almond orchards dot the countryside – but none more eye-catching, or sweeter, than the hand-made *frutti alla martorana*: garishly coloured fruits like peaches, oranges, grapes and prickly pears made from pure, sweet marzipan. These are a Sicilian speciality and take their name from the nuns of the convent at Palermo's La Martorana church, who first created them in 1233. The convent and the nuns are long gone but their marzipan extravagances live on and are traditionally given as gifts on All Souls' Day, the 2 November.

the slopes of Mount Etna. Some of the island's lemon harvest finds its way into *limoncello,* another syrupy after-dinner drink.

Wine

Sicilian wines have a great pedigree, dating back to Phoenician and Greek times, but have traditionally under-performed. With their prodigious amounts of sugar, they were dispatched north for blending, to bump up the strength of better-known wines. More recently, though, there has been a full-scale return to producing serious drinking wines, and to harnessing native grape varieties to that end. Good quality reds are made from the local Nero d'Avola grape variety; look out too for the dry red Cerasuolo di Vittoria

Classic Sicilian dessert of cannoli

from Ragusa province, the dry whites from Alcamo in the west and the up-and-coming new wines from the lava-enriched foothills of Etna.

NOTES

Sicily has seen an increasing number of wine estates where you can usually stay, dine or do a cookery or wine-tasting course. Outstanding examples are La Foresteria, on the Planeta estate outside Menfi, and Feudi del Pisciotto, near Niscemi.

Sicily's most famous wine – and long one of its most famous exports – is Marsala, a fortified wine comparable to port or sherry. It's been produced since the 18th century near the city on the southwestern coast from which it takes its name and is drunk as an aperitif or with/after dessert. A Marsala vergine rivals top sherries and ports. Restaurants in Marsala serve *Marsala all'uovo,* Marsala that has been blended with sugar and egg. If you find you like this particularly, as it is commercially produced you can find it in all shops and supermarkets.

Sweet elixirs, in fact, are something of a Sicilian speciality. Malvasia is another dessert wine made in the Aeolian Islands, and the island of Pantelleria produces Moscato di Pantelleria Naturale, made from Zibibbo grapes that are fermented in the sun. Taormina produces vino alla Mandorla, a wine made from almonds. Both are served after a meal with dessert.

Of course, Sicily also produces some excellent table wines. Many travellers may already be familiar with the island's red and white Corvos, which are exported around the world and are available throughout the island as well. Etna is produced from grapes grown on volcanic soil in the foothills of the volcano and is available as red, white or rosé. They tend to have a heavier and fruitier flavour. Some wines that are little known outside Sicily but are well worth looking for are Alcamo, from around Trapani, and Cerasuolo di Vittoria, from vineyards outside Ragusa.

MENU READER

Here are a few terms that may enhance your dining experiences. Be bold – your efforts at speaking Italian will be much appreciated.

Buona sera. Good afternoon/evening.
Parla inglese? Do you speak English?
Aperto Open
Chiuso Closed
Prima colazione Breakfast
Pranzo Lunch
Cena Dinner
Avete un menu? Do you have a menu?
Vorrei... I would like...

Sicilian reds are on the up

Quanto costa? How much is it?
Il conto, per favore. The bill, please.
Avete una tavola per una/due/tre/quattro persona/persone? Do you have a table for one/two/three/four people?

In addition to the regional specialities here are some common terms you are likely to encounter on Sicilian menus:

aglio garlic
agnello lamb
baccalaru Sicilian for *baccalà*, salted cod
basilico basil
birra beer
burro butter

caffè coffee
calamari squid
ceci chickpeas
cipolle onions
coniglio rabbit
cozze mussels
fagioli beans
finnochio fennel
formaggio cheese
frittata omelette
frutti di mare seafood
funghi mushrooms
gamberetti shrimp
insalata salad
maiale pork
melanzane aubergine
pane bread
panna cream
patate potatoes
peperoni peppers
pesce fish
polipo octopus
pollo chicken
pomodori tomatoes
prosciutto ham
spiedino skewers of meat
spinachi spinach
tè tea
uova eggs
vitello veal

Some typical pastas

fettucine long, flat, narrow strips
fusilli spiral-shaped pasta
orecchiette ear-shaped pasta
pappardelle wide, short noodles
penne short tubes
tagliatelle flat egg noodles
vermicelli thin spaghetti

Some common pasta sauces

aglio e olio with garlic, oil, light chilli
alla Norma with eggplant
arrabbiata hot tomato sauce
ragù meat sauce, what the English call bolognese
napolitana with tomato and basil
pesto a mixture of basil, garlic, and pine nuts
vongole with clams, garlic and oil

Places to eat

Price for a two-course meal for one person, including a glass of wine and service charge:
€€€€ = over 50 euros
€€€ = 30–50 euros
€€ = 20–30 euros
€ = below 20 euros

Palermo

Antica Focacceria San Francesco Via Paternostro 58; www.anticafocacceria.it. For a century and a half, this Palermo institution has been serving tasty, baked-on-the-premises focaccia bread and other rustic snacks from its high-ceilinged, marble-floored location. You can easily assemble a meal from the sandwiches, *arancine* (fried rice balls) and other fare, and enjoy it in colourful surroundings. **€€**

Osteria dei Vespri Piazza Croce dei Vespri 6; www.osteriadeivespri.it. This old tavern occupies the ex-coach house of the 18th-century Palazzo Gangi on a lovely, sheltered square with outdoor tables in summer. The cooking is creative Italian, with artfully presented dishes and a fantastic selection of wines to boot. **€€€€**

I Cuochini Via Ruggero Settimo 68; www.icuochini.com. Diminutive, spick-and-span *frigittoria* – all gleaming white tiles and zinc – founded in 1826, and concealed within an arched gateway (the only sign is a small ceramic plaque). *Panzerotti* (deep-fried pastries, stuffed with tomato, mozzarella and anchovy, or aubergine, courgette and cheese), *arancini* (with *ragù*, or cheese and ham), *pasticcino* (a sweet pastry with minced meat), *timballini di pasta* (deep-fried pasta), *besciamelle fritte* (breadcrumbed and deep-fried *béchamel*) and the like most at less than €1 a portion. **€**

Trattoria Torremuzza Via Torremuzza 17; 091 252 5532. Eat at streetside tables in summer at this bustling, no-frills trattoria where fish is grilled on an outside brazier. There is a huge set menu including rough house wine, or plump for a mussel soup or pasta with mussels and clams, or swordfish and aubergine. **€€**

Pizzeria Italia Via Orologio 54; www.ristorantepizzeriaitalia.it. Attracting large queues, this is a great choice for light, oven-blistered pizzas. Try the "*Palermitana*" with tomato, anchovies, onion, artichokes, caciocavallo cheese and breadcrumbs. **€€**

Aeolian Islands (Isole Eolie)

La Lampara Via Vittorio Emanuele, Stromboli; www.lalamparastromboli.com. Dine on the large, raised terrace beneath a pergola of climbing vines among huge pots of basil and rosemary. Dishes include pizza, pasta and grilled meat and fish. **€€€**

Filippino Piazza Municipio, Lípari; www.filippino.it. This stupendous fish restaurant – Lipari's best, in business since 1910 – is in the upper town and has a shaded outdoor terrace where you can eat classy Aeolian specialities like borlotti bean, sardine and fennel soup, *risotto nero*, grouper-stuffed *ravioloni* and local fish in a tomato sauce. They also have a great selection of inventive desserts. **€€€€**

Da Alfredo Piazza Marina Garibaldi, Lingua, Salina; www.facebook.com/DaAlfredosalina/. Right on the seafront piazza, this little café is known for its fresh fruit granitas – the summer yachties and boat-trippers queue up for a taste, while Dolce and Gabbana and Naomi Campbell have been known to drop by. Their other speciality is *pane cunzato*, a huge round of grilled bread piled with various combinations of home-cured tuna, capers, tomatoes, baked ricotta and olives. One between two will satisfy most. **€**

Paperò Via Rotabile, Rinella, Salina; www.facebook.com/salinapapero. Run with verve and passion by three siblings, this friendly bar does a great *tavola calda* of home-cooked food (and yummy cakes for afterwards). A great hangout at any time of day, but especially in the evening, when you can sit on the terrace and watch the sun set. Do not miss the ricotta granita scattered with candied capers, caper salt and fresh mint. **€**

Agrigento

Antica Panelleria Musicò Viale della Vittoria s/n. This little van parked at the beginning of Viale della Vittoria is an Agrigento institution, selling *pane e panelle* (chickpea flour fritters in soft bread rolls) since 1954. **€**

Ex Panificio Piazza Giuseppe Sinatra; www.osteriaexpanificio.it. Lovely and very popular place occupying the premises of a historic bakery where the focus is on carefully sourced ingredients. Try ravioli stuffed with local goat cheese, spaghetti with anchovies and breadcrumbs or *cavatelli alla norma* (with tomato, salted ricotta and aubergine). They also have a tantalising cocktail list, so come here for your aperitivo as well. **€€€**

Catania

Antica Marina Via Pardo 29; www.anticamarina.it. Trattoria buzzing with old fashioned atmosphere bang in the heart of the fish market where you can eat reasonably priced, fresh fish on tables laid with paper cloths. Go for one of the set menus – a mixed antipasto plus two kinds of pasta or an antipasto plus mixed fried fish, a lemon sorbet and coffee. **€€**

Me Cumpari Turiddu Via Ventimiglia 15; www.mecumparituriddu.it/en/. One for the foodies. Rigorously sourced ingredients in simple, intelligent dishes. Try the *sformato* of spiny artichokes (a local delicacy), deep-fried ricotta with Salina capers, olives and an orange sauce, or the home-made pasta with a sauce of Nebrodi black pork. **€€€**

Piazza Scammacca Piazza Scammacca 9; www.piazzascammacca.com. Cool and lively food mall in a distinctly Sicilian key, occupying the ground floor of an 18th century palazzo in the heart of Catania. There are four food 'stalls', each with its own specialty – seafood, panini, flame-grilled steak, pizza – a café (that does great cocktails) and a wine bar. **€€**

Cefalù

Caffè di Noto Via Bagno Cicerone 3. This gelateria, on the edge of the centro storico and the beginning of the Lungomare, has fabulous ice creams in flavours including Sicilian mango, raspberry, prickly pear, and chocolate with chilli, and for the adventurous, seawater and lemon granita. **€**

Le Chat Noir Via XXV Novembre 17; www.ristorantelechatnoir.it. An atmospheric setting in the whitewashed, plant-filled courtyard of a sixteenth-century building a short walk from the Duomo. The menu features memorable executions of Sicilian dishes such as aubergine *parmigiana* with salty ricotta, swordfish *involtini* and an orange salad spiked with chilli. **€€**

Tivitti Via Lungomare G Giardina 7; www.bottegativitti.it. Contemporary twist on a traditional wine bar with wines by the bottle or glass (including antipasti nibbles), as well as excellent pizzas, many of them using local produce and ingredients such as *Madonie* white truffles to great effect. There are also hamburgers using Sicilian beef served with tasty combinations of sundried tomatoes, local cheeses and olives. For a beach picnic, buy a bottle and cold cuts to take away. There are tables inside and out, overlooking the beach. **€€**

Enna

Umbriaco Viale IV Novembre 11; www.umbriaco1974.it. In this tiny, but chic, little shop on the outskirts of Enna, Rosario Umbriaco creates what will probably be the best *arancini* – stuffed, deep-fried balls of rice – you will ever experience. Try the double layered *arancino*. The first layer is flavoured with saffron and wild mint, the second layer with fresh ricotta, parsley and black pepper, and the centre is filled with melted black pepper and saffron scented *piacentinu ennese* cheese. **€**

Erice

Caffè Maria Via Vittorio Emanuele 4; www.caffe-maria.vmv-web.it. Don't leave town without a visit to the café or its sister *pasticceria* a few doors down, for marzipan goodies and exquisite cannoli. The café's founder, Maria Grammatico, learned her trade as a girl in a convent, and has co-written a recipe book with writer Mary Taylor Simeti. **€**

La Pentolaccia Via Guarnotti 17; www.ristorantelapentolaccia.it. Atmospherically housed in an old monastery, this moderately priced place serves excellent home-made pasta and couscous. Try the ravioli stuffed with *cernia* (grouper) in a sauce of cherry tomato, swordfish, mint and prawns. **€€€**

Módica

Accursio Ristorante Via Grimaldi 41, Módica Alta; www.accursioristorante.it/en/. This Michelin-starred restaurant run by renowned chef Accursio Craparo serves Sicilian fare with a modern twist. Early booking recommended. They also run the less expensive wine bar next door, *Radici*, where the food is similarly excellent. **€€€€**

Osteria dei Sapori Perduti Corso Umberto 1 228–230; www.osteriadeisaporiperduti.it. Marvellous value, right on the Corso, where you can eat reasonably priced traditional rustic dishes, inside or out, with an emphasis on beans and pulses. The abundant mixed antipasto is a good way to start, and enough for two people, followed by *lolli con le fave* (handmade pasta with fava bean purée). There are also a good selection of traditional desserts (cassata, cannoli or pistachio semi freddo). The menu is in Sicilian, but translations are available. **€€**

Noto

Trattoria Baglieri Il Crocifisso Via Principe Umberto 46; www.ristorante crocifisso.it. Nationally recognized super-chic trattoria using seasonal local ingredients in ways that make the taste buds zing: spaghetti with white prawns and Siracusan lemon, rabbit with orange blossom honey, wild greens, celery, carrot and peppers, tuna in a pistachio and sesame crust. **€€€€**

Trattoria del Carmine Via Ducezio 9. Everything at this simple, family-run trattoria is fresh and homemade. Regional specialities include seafood-based pastas and *coniglio alla stimpirate*, a traditional Sicilian rabbit dish with a sweet and sour sauce. **€€**

Piazza Armerina

Da Totò Via Mazzini 29; www.ristorantedatoto.net. This pleasant, family-run trattoria in the heart of Piazza Armerina is an excellent place to stop for fresh pasta and seafood mains when passing through town en route to Villa Romana in nearby Casale. **€€**

Ragusa

I Banchi Via Orfanotrofio 39; www.ibanchiragusa.it. Styled as a "basilica of taste" by its creator, Ciccio Sultano of Duomo (see below). At the root of it all is their fantastic home-made bread and pasta, along with meticulously sourced deli produce – all on sale. Then there's café-style service for traditional (but exceptional) street food and pastries; and a more sophisticated set lunch. **€€**

Ristorante Duomo Via Capitano Bocchieri 31; Ragusa Ibla; www.cicciosultano.it. Meticulously sourced Sicilian ingredients reworked to stunning effect – black truffle ice cream, a savoury cannolo with a dab of caviar, for example – in what is arguably Sicily's greatest restaurant. Put yourself in the hands of chef Ciccio Sultano, and opt for one of the tasting menus. **€€€€**

Ristorante Locanda Don Serafino Via Orfanotrofio 39, Ragusa Ibla; www.locandadonserafino.it. In an atmospheric vaulted medieval wine cellar, lit by candles, this is a place to feast on simple, well-executed dishes like handmade black spaghetti with squid ink, squid and ricotta, or an Angus steak with roasted vegetables and a red pepper ketchup. There are also several themed tasting menus and a good value three-course lunch menu. **€€€€**

Siracusa

Fratelli Burgio Piazza Cesare Battisti 4; www.fratelliburgio.com. A mecca for foodies, this deli in the heart of the market is the place to come for artisan, DOP and Slow Food Presidio cheeses and cured meats from all over Italy. Look out for speck matured in myrtleberry grappa, a Sicilian *suino nero prosciutto crudo* from the Nebrodi mountains, handmade salami from Trentino's Val di Non or a blue buffalo-milk cheese from Piemonte. At lunchtime they serve a range of cheeses, cold meats and condiments on wooden platters – best savoured with a glass of chilled white wine eaten on tables outside amid the bustle of the market. **€€**

Oz & Cappuccio Via Giaracà 8; www.facebook.com/ozecappuccio. Joint venture between a musician from Berlin and the son of the market's biggest fishmongers. There's no booking, and no frills, just spanking fresh fish served in biodegradable cardboard boxes at little tables. Wine made by Oz on his vineyard outside Siracusa goes down a treat too. Try the super-crispy mixed fried fish (squid, anchovies and prawns), or the tuna burger. Expect to queue, but pass the time while you are waiting with a glass of Oz's rose. **€€**

Taormina

Al Duomo Vico Ebrei 1; www.ristorantealduomotaormina.com. In the heart of the town this is an atmospheric, reliable restaurant with a rustic-chic interior and a sought-after terrace overlooking Piazza Duomo. Try the hearty seafood cuisine, fresh fish or casseroled lamb and end with the *tortino di cioccolato* dessert. **€€€**

Pizzeria Romana Via dei Cappuccini 1; www.villazuccaro.com/la-romana. Bustling pizzeria where the service is as fast as greased-lightening, and the pizzas come light, blistered and generously topped with interesting combinations such as the Nocina with hazelnut cream, gorgonzola and mozzarella and the Fichi e Prosciutto with parma ham and roast fresh figs. **€**

Trattoria da Nino Via Luigi Pirandello 37; www.trattoriadaninotaormina.com. Welcoming place that, despite its touristy appearance, is popular with locals: the mixed vegetable or mixed fish antipasti are particularly good – and enough for a light lunch for two. There are plenty of reasonably priced primi. **€€**

Wunderbar Café Piazza IX Aprile; www.wunderbarcaffe.com. Once the haunt of Garbo and Fassbinder, this is the place to splash out on an Aperol Spritz at aperitif time or an after-dinner drink for a touch of Taormina people-watching. They also serve classic Sicilian breakfasts and lunch and dinner. **€€€€**

Travel essentials

Practical information

Accessible travel

Most churches and sites have steps, though an increasing number of museums and archaeological sites have wheelchair access. Hotels are required to have at least one accessible room, though establishments located in historical buildings may not be wheelchair accessible.

Accommodation

Sicily has plentiful accommodation ranging from luxurious grand hotels,stylish boutique and country house hotels, to simple B&Bs and privately rented apartments. Accommodation in the interior is thinner on the ground, with the notable exception of the southeast where there is a swathe of superb hotels in and around Siracusa, Ragusa, Modica and Scicli. Book ahead, especially at Easter and in summer, as most hotels use dynamic pricing (which tariffs rocket when demand is high). Many resorts close in winter; some hotels or farm stays insist on half or full board in high season.

Agriturismi or farmstays have improved dramatically and are generally delightful and good value. To be labelled an *agriturismo* the property must earn most of its income from agricultural pursuits. Meals will more often than not feature home-grown ingredients. Villa rentals is now big business thanks to foreign villa-owners and design-conscious locals – as well as reputable villa specialists abroad.

I'd like a single/double bed. **Vorrei una camera singola/ matrimoniale** or **doppia.**
With bath/shower **Con bagno/doccia**
What is the price per night? **Qual è il prezzo per una notte?**

Airports

Sicily has four airports: Palermo (Falcone-Borsellino), Catania (Fontanarossa), Trapani (Birgi) and Comiso (Pio la Torre). The main international airports are Palermo and Catania; international flights operated by low-cost airlines sometimes use Trapani and Comiso – though this changes from year to year.

Palermo's **Aeroporto Falcone Borsellino** (www.gesap.it) is 30km (18 miles) west of the city at Punta Raisi. Buses run every half hour from 5am to the time of the last arrival of the day to Palermo's Piazza Politeama and the central train station. The journey time is 45 minutes to an hour. The Trinacria Express train service, which also runs every half hour from the airport to the central station, takes 55 minutes and is a fraction cheaper than the bus.

Catania's **Aeroporto Fontanarossa** (www.aeroporto.catania.it) is 5km (3 miles) south of the city. Buses leave from outside the terminal for the 20-minute trip to Piazza Stesicoro in the centre of the city and to Stazione Centrale, departing roughly every 20 minutes from 5am to midnight. Buses from the airport also make connections to Siracusa, Ragusa, Taormina and many other cities in eastern Sicily, as well as Palermo.

Trápani-Birgi's Aeroporto **Vincenzo Florio** (www.airgest.it), used by low-cost domestic carriers and sometimes international carriers, is 15km (9 miles) southeast of Trápani. AST buses link the airport to the town every half hour, taking 25 minutes. Salvatore Lumia buses link the airport with Agrigento and Salemi buses with Palermo and Marsala.

The **Aeroporto di Comiso Pio la Torre** (www.aeroportodicomiso.eu), 5km (3 miles) north of Comiso, is used by low-cost carriers and Alitalia. AST buses connect the airport with Ragusa while several other bus companies link the airport with Agrigento, Modica and Catania.

When is the next plane to…? **A che ora parte il prossimo aereo per…?**
I would like a ticket for… **Vorrei un biglietto per…**
Please take these bags to the train/bus/taxi. **Mi porti queste valige fino al treno/all'autobus/al taxi, per favore.**

Apps

The Trenitalia app allows you to book train tickets and check on delays direct from your phone. The Liberty Lines app is similarly useful if you are island hopping. Uber is becoming increasingly common in larger cities.

Camping

Camping is permitted only in designated sites, of which there are about 90 in Sicily. Most are on the coast and Egadi Islands.

Car Hire

Most major companies such as Avis, Hertz and Europcar have outlets at the airports but it is usually cheaper to book in advance. Inclusive' prices do not generally include personal accident insurance or insurance against damage to windscreens, tyres and wheels. For renting, the minimum age is usually 25. Drivers must present their own national driving licence or one that is internationally recognised. Credit card imprints are taken as a deposit and are usually the only form of payment acceptable.

Climate

Sicily enjoys good weather year-round, with mild winters and hot summers. The only extremes you can expect are in July and August, when daytime temperatures of 40°C (95°F) are not unusual. The southern coast is the warmest place on the island, and it is often buffeted by hot sirocco winds that blow in off the Sahara. November and December can be rainy and expect the occasional shower until March. Spring arrives early and the island is unusually pleasant at this time because wildflowers bloom everywhere. Below are average temperatures in Palermo, accurate for most of the island except in the cooler mountainous interior and on the southern coast in the summer.

	J	F	M	A	M	J	J	A	S	O	N	D
°C	10.5	10.5	13	16	18.5	23	25.5	25	23	20	17	12.5
°F	52	52	55	61	73	78	77	73	68	62	62	56

Crime and Safety

Leave passports, jewellery, large amounts of cash, credit cards you are not using and other valuables in the hotel safe (many hotels provide them in the rooms; if not, ask to check in valuables at the desk). Keep a copy of your passport and other valuable documents separately in case you need to replace them. Be particularly vigilant at markets, street festivals and other occasions where large crowds congregate.

Never leave valuables in view within your car; whenever possible, park in an attended lot (most archaeological sites and other attractions have them). To protect yourself against Vespa-riding bandits, who snatch bags while whizzing by at high speed, carry your bag so it faces away from the street.

If you are robbed, report it as soon as possible to the local police. You will need a copy of the declaration in order to claim on your insurance.

I want to report a theft. **Voglio denunciare un furto.**
My wallet/passport/ticket has been stolen. **Mi hanno rubato il portafoglio/il passaporto/il biglietto.**

Driving

A car in Sicily is a great help for exploring the island, though in cities like Palermo, Catania or Siracusa, it is easier and less nerve-wracking to use public transport or taxis. The network of roads has much improved though you can still expect potholes even on some of the major roads, and if you are exploring well off-the-beaten-track, you may come across unsurfaced country roads (*strada sterrata*). A system of mainly toll-free motorways (*autostrade*) crosses parts of the island, linking the main cities. Elsewhere, roads can be quite slow-going, especially in the mountainous regions. The main frustrations of driving in Sicily are negotiating town centres (which often have complex one-way systems and poor signing to the centre), finding parking places in town centres and keeping your cool with fellow motorists who drive fast and frequently recklessly.

Curva pericolosa Dangerous curve
Deviazione Detour (diversion)
Divieto di sorpasso No passing (overtaking)

Divieto di sosta No stopping
Lavori in corso Men working (road works)
Pericolo Danger
Rallentare Slow down
Senso vietato/unico No entry/one-way street
Vieto l'ingresso No entry
Zona pedonale Pedestrian zone
Zona traffico limita Limited traffic zone

Rules and Regulations. The speed limit on motorways is 130km/h (80mph), secondary roads is 90km/h (55mph); in towns, it's 50km/h (30mph). Drive on the right, overtake on the left. At intersections and traffic circles (roundabouts), traffic on the right has the right of way. Speeding and other traffic offences are subject to heavy on-the-spot fines. The use of hand-held mobiles while driving is prohibited. The blood alcohol limit is 0.05 percent, and police occasionally make random breath tests. Lights must be used on all out-of-town roads.

Breakdowns and Assistance. In case of an accident or breakdown, dial 113 (general emergency) or the Automobile Club of Italy on 116. Roadside phones are placed at frequent intervals along major roads.

Parking. Historic centres are often inaccessible to cars, other than those of residents, though visitors staying at hotels with parking facilities are allowed access. Many Sicilian cities and towns have municipal parking lots and garages, denoted by a white 'P' on a blue background, at the fringes of their historic centres; use these whenever possible. Electric charge points are becoming increasingly common.

Fuel. Petrol *(benzina)* is readily available and there are many 24-hour stations with self-service dispensers that accept euro notes and credit cards.

Driver's licence **Patente**
Car registration papers **Libretto di circolazione**
Green insurance card **Carte verde**

Can I park here? **Posso parcheggiare qui?**
Are we on the right road for…? **Siamo sulla strada giusta per…?**
I've had a breakdown. **Ho avuto un guasto.**
There's been an accident. **C'è stato un incidente.**

Electricity

220V/50Hz is standard. Visitors from other countries may require an adaptor *(una presa complementare)*, and those from North America will need a converter as well. Connections are either two or three round-pins. Adaptors can be found locally, but it is wiser to carry an international adaptor. Better hotels often have special outlets for some North American appliances.

Embassies and Consulates

In Rome:

Australian Embassy http://italy.embassy.gov.au
Canadian Embassy www.international.gc.ca/country-pays/splash/italy-italie.aspx?lang=eng
Irish Embassy: www.dfa.ie/irish-embassy/italy
UK Embassy: www.gov.uk/world/organisations/british-embassy-rome
US Embassy: https://it.usembassy.gov

Emergencies

The general emergency number is 113. Call 112 for police, 115 for fire and 118 for an ambulance. For road assistance dial 116.

Please, can you place an emergency call for me to the…? **Per favore, mi può fare una telefonata d'emergenza…?**
police **alla polizia**
Fire! **Al fuoco!**
fire brigade **ai pompieri**

ambulance **ambulanza**
hospital **al'ospedale**

Getting There

By Air. Major European cities have direct flights to Sicily. From the UK direct services are operated by British Airways from Gatwick to Catania and from Heathrow to Palermo; low-cost carrier Easyjet flies to Palermo from London Gatwick and to Catania from Gatwick, Luton, Bristol and Manchester; Ryanair from Stansted to Palermo and Catania. From New York there are twice weekly flights direct to Palermo operated by ITA (www.ita-airways.com). Other flights from North America, and from Australia and New Zealand, fly to Rome or Milan or a major hub elsewhere in Europe with onward connections to Palermo or Catania.

By Rail. The Italian mainland is linked to Sicily by train, with Milan, Rome and Naples the best connecting stations to the south. Unfortunately, the great improvements in the Italian rail system do not extend to Sicily, and the overnight sleeper service from Sicily to northern Italy has been cancelled.

There is a regular daily service between Rome and Palermo, Catania and Siracusa. At the crossing from Villa San Giovanni on the Italian peninsula the train carriages are shunted into the ferry, and then shunted off again at Messina. Palermo's main station is Stazione Centrale. Always book a seat for long-distance travel. Credit card bookings can be made online (www.trenitalia.com) or go through any local travel agent.

By Sea. Ferries link Sicily with Naples, Genova (Genoa), Salerno and Civitavecchia in Italy and with Cagliari in Sardinia; there are also links with Malta. Hydrofoils *(aliscafi)* operate between Sicily and its smaller islands (see page 139).

Ferry tickets can be booked online (though there is no need for the Messina/Villa San Giovanni crossing). The main operators are SNAV (www.snav.it), Grandi Navi Veloci (www.gnv.it), Tirrenia (www.tirrenia.it) and Grimaldi (www.grimaldi-lines.com). There are cabins on the longer routes, and these must be booked well in advance for high summer. Remember that sailing schedules are prone to change, especially in winter months when the seas can turn rough. Hydrofoils are run by Liberty Lines (www.libertylines.it).

By Car. Driving to Sicily from the UK takes 24 hours at the very least, with most people choosing to take several days over the journey. Even from Rome it is a good seven hours to Villa San Giovanni in Calabria, where you cross to Sicily. To bring a car into Italy you will need a current driving licence and valid insurance. You must carry your driving licence, car registration, insurance documents and passport with you at all times when driving. You are also required to carry a triangular warning sign and a visibility vest.

Guides and Tours

Guides are readily available in Sicily's cities and at its archaeological sites to provide tours in English though prices are high for small groups.

I would like an English-speaking guide. **Ho bisogno di una guida chi parla inglese.**

Health and Medical Care

Non-EU residents should have travel insurance to cover all eventualities. You will often be asked to pay for treatment up front, so keep all receipts for reimbursement. In many areas in summer there is a *Guardia Medica Turistica* (tourist emergency medical service) which functions 24 hours a day. Details are available from pharmacies, tourist offices, hotels and local newspapers.

Pharmacies *(farmacie)* have green cross signs above the entrance; in each town, one stays open late and on Sundays on a rotating basis. The after-hour locations for the month are posted in all pharmacies. For serious cases or emergencies, dial 118 for an ambulance or head for the *Pronto Soccorso* (Accident and Emergency) of the local hospital.

I need a doctor/dentist. **Ho bisogno di un medico/dentista.**
I have a stomachache. **Ho mal di stomaco.**
I have sunstroke. **Ho una colpo di sole.**

Language

Many Sicilians speak Italian and Sicilian, which is a rich blend of Italian and the languages of the various powers who have invaded the island over the centuries; Arabic, French, and Spanish words appear regularly. English is spoken in hotels and restaurants, but once you venture off the tourist track, prepare to communicate in Italian. Here are some basic tips:

a as in *father*

e as in *egg*

i as *e* in *eat*

o as in *ostracise*

u as *oo* in *mood*

c before *e* and *i* is pronounced *ch*, as in *church*. Otherwise, *c* and *ch* are pronounced *k*, as in *cane*.

g before *e* and *i* is pronounced *j*, as in *gin*. Before other letters, *g* is hard, as in *gun*.

Most feminine words end in *a*, plural *e*, and most masculine words end in *o*, plural *i*. *La* is the feminine article, *il* the masculine.

Some basic words and phrases:

Good morning/good afternoon. **Buon giorno.** bwon JOARno

Please. **Per favore.** pair fahVOAray

Thank you. **Grazie.** GRAAseeay

yes/no **sì/no** see/no

Excuse me. **Mi scusi.** mi skoozee

Where is…? **Dovè…?** doaVAI…?

I don't understand. **Non capisco.** noan kahpeeskoa

open **aperto** ahPAIRtoe

closed **chiuso** keeOOso

Days of the week:

Monday **lunedì**

Tuesday **martedì**

Wednesday **mercoledì**

Thursday **giovedì**

Friday **venerdì**

Saturday **sabato**
Sunday **domenica**
Numbers:
one **uno**
two **due**
three **tre**
four **quattro**
five **cinque**
six **sei**
seven **sette**
eight **otto**
nine **nove**
ten **diece**
hundred **cento**

LGBTQ+ Travellers

Attitudes are fairly relaxed, and gay magazines are sold at most newsstands. Taormina is still the flamboyant focus for the native and foreign LGBTQ+ community, but there are LGTBQ+ scenes in all the bigger towns and many seaside resorts.

Money

Currency. The unit of currency in Italy is the euro, written as €. Notes are denominated in 5, 10, 20, 50, 100 and 500; coins in 1 and 2 euros and 1, 2, 5, 10, 20 and 50 cents. Contactless payments are fast becoming the norm, though you should always have some cash handy. Although you can take euros out from cash machines directly from your home account, it is cheaper to load money onto an international digital account, such as Wise (www.wise.com) which can provide you with a digital or physical contactless card.

Opening Hours

Museums and monuments throughout Sicily are remaining open longer than they once did, often seven days a week and into the early evening.

Even so, hours vary widely. Smaller museums may open mornings only, or mornings and just for a couple of afternoons a week. Many museums and sites are closed on Monday. Most churches open early, around 7am or 8am for Mass, close at noon, then open again for two or three hours at 4pm or 5pm; but don't be surprised to find churches closed for ongoing restorations, and that major sites can close without warning. Some museums and archaeological sites are closed on Mondays. Local tourist boards can provide current opening times for sights in a particular town or region.

Banks. Generally open Mon–Fri 8.30am–1.30pm. Some are open in the afternoon 2.30–4pm or 3–4.30pm.

Shops and businesses. Although an increasing number of shops are staying open all day, traditional opening times are Mon–Sat 8 or 9am–1pm and 4–7.30pm.

Restaurants. Usually open 12.30–3pm or 3.30pm for lunch and from 8–10.30pm for dinner (closed one day a week).

Police

There are three kinds of police in Italy: *vigili urbani*, who deal with petty crime, traffic, parking and other day-to-day matters; *carabinieri*, the highly trained national force who handle serious crime and civilian unrest, protect government figures and perform other high-profile tasks; and *polizia stradale*, who patrol the roadways. Any of these forces may answer a 113 emergency call, though the *carabinieri* have their own emergency number, 112.

Where's the nearest police station? **Dovè il più vicino posto di polizia?**

Public Holidays

Sicily celebrates local festivals throughout the year (see page 104), and all of the national holidays as well. These are:

1 January New Year's Day *(Capodanno)*

6 January Epiphany *(Befana)*

Spring Easter Sunday and Monday *(Pasqua)*
25 April Liberation Day *(Anniversario della Liberazione)*
1 May Labour Day *(Festa del Lavoro)*
15 August *Ferragosto* and Assumption Day
1 November All Saints Day *(Ognisanti)*
8 December Day of the Immaculate Conception *(Immacolata)*
25 December Christmas *(Natale)*
26 December St Stephen's Day *(Santo Stefano)*

Telephone

For calls within Italy, telephone numbers must be preceded by the full area code even if the call is made within the same district. When phoning abroad form Italy dial 00, then the country code, followed by the city or area code and the number (omitting any initial 0). International dialling codes are 1 for the US and Canada, 44 for the UK, 353 for the Republic of Ireland, 61 for Australia, 64 for New Zealand. Hotels slap very large surcharges on long-distance calls.

Mobile (Cell) Phones. Check the international roaming rates with your provider prior to departure, and whether your phone can receive and make calls in Italy. Roaming rates are generally high for non-EU countries and if you are making a lot of calls or staying for some time it may be worth purchasing a SIM 'pay as you go' card available from many tobacconists as well as from the main providers (Wind, Tre, Tim).

Time Zones

Like the rest of Italy, Sicily is on Central European Time, that is one hour ahead of Greenwich Mean Time (gmt). Italy switches to daylight saving time on the last Sunday in March and reverts to standard time on the last Sunday in October.

New York	**Sicily**	Jo'burg	Sydney	Auckland
7am	**noon**	1pm	9pm	11p

Tipping

In Italy a service charge of 10–15 percent is usually built into the bill, though a little extra for good service is always appreciated. At a bar, it is customary to leave a coin or two on the counter for a barman. Tip bellhops one euro per bag. To tip a taxi driver, simply round up the total.

Toilets

Public restrooms can be hard to find, and when you do locate one, you usually have to pay to use it. Toilets in cafés and bars can be used by the public but buying a drink at the same time will be appreciated. The mens' restroom is designated by *uomini* or *signori,* the ladies' by *donne* or *signore.* Major sites now have reasonable facilities but those in train and bus stations are not always well maintained.

Is it possible to use the bathroom? **Posso usare il bagno?**
Where are the toilets? **Dove sono i gabinetti?**

Transport

Coach and Bus

Fast bus services, operated by various different companies, link Sicily's main towns and offer relatively speedy access to the interior and the south. Generally speaking, coaches are more reliable and quicker than trains, but they cost more. City buses have a flat fare and tickets are valid for 75 minutes, including change of bus routes. Services are limited on Sundays, and in many cases, after the late afternoon. Bus tickets, available from bars, tobacconists, and from machines at bus terminals and metro stations, must be validated in the machine on the bus. Tourist offices can provide bus schedules and fare information.

Ferries and Hydrofoils

Aeolian Islands: Ferries and hydrofoils run regularly from Milazzo on the northern coast near Messina. Boats run year-round to all the islands with the most extensive service in the summer (in peak season there are up to

11 hydrofoils a day to Lípari and Vulcano, and six a day to Salina). There are direct ferries to the islands several times a week, but all can best be reached through Lípari. Off-season boats can be cancelled due to inclement weather.

Egadi Islands: Trápani on the western coast is the port for ferries and hydrofoils to the Egadi Islands (Favignana, Lévanzo and Marettimo) and Pantelleria.

Ferries to the islands are mainly operated by Liberty Lines (www.libertylines.it).

Rail

Trains are operated by Italian State Railways, Ferrovie dello Stato (www.trenitalia.com). The rail system in Sicily is cheap but slow and not really convenient for seeing all of the island. The east of the island is better linked than the west. Messina is well linked to both Palermo and Catania, and all trains to Italy pass through its port in order to cross the Strait of Messina by ferry. Catania is linked with the major cities (though trains take twice as long from here to Palermo as the coach) and is the starting point of the Ferrovia Circumetnea, the narrow-gauge train that calls at all villages around Mount Etna on a circular route. Seat reservations are obligatory on the faster Intercity services. Tickets for all trains must be stamped in the yellow machines on the platforms before boarding the train. Failure to do so can incur a hefty on-the-spot fine.

Taxi

In cities, taxis are best telephoned or found at taxi ranks in the main squares of the larger towns. Licensed taxis are white, with a Taxi sign on the roof, and have a meter which should be turned on at the start of the journey. Beware of touts without meters who may approach you at airports and large train stations.

Palermo: Radio Taxi: tel: 091 513311; 091 513198.

Catania: Radio Taxi: tel: 095 330966.

When is the next bus/train to…? **Quando parte il prossimo autobus/treno per…?**
one way **andata**

roundtrip **andata e ritorno**
first/second class **prima/seconda classe**
What's the fare to...? **Qual è la tariffa per...?**

Visas and Entry Requirements

Citizens of EU countries need only a valid passport or an identity card to enter Italy. British citizens need a valid passport with at least three months left before expiry. Citizens of the US, Canada, Australia, New Zealand and South Africa need only a valid passport, though a special visa or resident permit is required for stays of more than 90 days. To facilitate the replacement process in case you lose your passport while travelling, photocopy the first page of your passport twice; leave one copy at home and keep another with you, but separately from the passport.

EU regulations now allow for the free exchange of goods for personal use between member countries. For residents of non-EU countries, the following restrictions apply:

IVA. A Value Added Tax of 22 percent is added to all purchases in Italy. Residents of non-EU countries can claim a refund for part of this tax on purchases of more than about €155 at stores participating in the VAT-refund scheme. The store will issue you a refund document, which you can redeem at the airport once you present your receipt to customs and have it stamped.

Websites

Useful sites are:

www.enit.it Italian government Tourist Board, covering all of Italy.

www.visitsicily.info Official Sicilian tourist website.

www.parks.it Italian parks and reserves (then consult Sicily).

www.bestofsicily.com packed with information on the island; strong on culture.

www.visitpalermo.it All about Palermo.

www.thethinkingtraveller.com Villas in Sicily, plus a useful and insightful guide to the island.

Index

THE **MINI** ROUGH GUIDE TO **SICILY**

First Edition 2025

Editor: Beth Williams
Author: Ros Belford
Picture Manager: Tom Smyth
Cartography Update: Katie Bennett
Layout: Ankur Guha
Production Operations Manager: Katie Bennett
Publishing Technology Manager: Rebeka Davies
Head of Publishing: Sarah Clark
Photography Credits: Fotolia 114; Insight Guides 39, 70, 86, 96, 101; Neil Buchan-Grant/Apa Publications 12BR, 21, 23, 24, 26, 34, 36, 37, 40, 43, 44, 45, 47, 50, 52, 54, 56, 58, 61, 62, 65, 66, 67, 69, 73, 74, 76, 81, 85, 89, 92, 97, 99, 102, 116; Public domain 31; Shutterstock 1, 4, 7, 9, 11, 12TL 12TR, 12CL, 12BL, 12CR, 13T, 13CT, 13CB, 13B, 14T, 14CL, 14BL, 14BR, 16T, 16CL, 16BL, 16BR, 18T, 18CL, 18BL, 18BR, 29, 32, 48, 60, 64, 79, 82, 91, 94, 104, 107, 109, 110, 112
Cover Credits: Syracuse **iStock**

About the author

Ros Belford co-authored the first edition of the Rough Guide to Italy, and has since written and broadcasted extensively about Italy and the Mediterranean. She lives in Cambridge and spends as much time as she can in Siracusa and on the Aeolian island of Salina.

Distribution

UK, Ireland and Europe: Apa Publications (UK) Ltd; sales@roughguides.com
United States and Canada: Ingram Publisher Services; ips@ingramcontent.com
Australia and New Zealand: Booktopia; retailer@booktopia.com.au
Worldwide: Apa Publications (UK) Ltd; sales@roughguides.com

Special Sales, Content Licensing and CoPublishing

Rough Guides can be purchased in bulk quantities at discounted prices. We can create special editions, personalised jackets and corporate imprints tailored to your needs.
sales@roughguides.com; http://roughguides.com

Printed in Czech Republic

This book was produced using **Typefi** automated publishing software.

Contact us

Every effort has been made to provide accurate information in this publication, but changes are inevitable. The publisher cannot be held responsible for any resulting loss, inconvenience or injury sustained by any traveller as a result of information or advice contained in the guide. We would appreciate it if readers would call our attention to any errors or outdated information, or if you feel we've left something out. Please send your comments with the subject line "Rough Guide Mini Sicily Update" to mail@uk.roughguides.com.